## Testimonials for The Sustainable High ROI

"I can't believe I have worked at the executive level in nonprofits for so long without this book as a reference. It's so practical and accessible."

*Christine Duncan MSW*
*CEO, YWCA Monterey County*

"Reading this book convinced me that getting and having more money does not mean overextended nonprofit leaders have to do more. I learned we do need to think differently about fundraising than the typical books advise. I've been involved with nonprofits for over 40 years and the *Sustainable High ROI Fundraising System* gave me new, fresh, and importantly, proven, ways to put an effective net-revenue-generating system in place. Every executive director needs to learn, using Joanne's approach, how they can absolutely work less and get more! The real-life cases using her system synched it for me. I'm excited to share this incredibly valuable book with nonprofit executive directors, board members, and colleagues."

*Mary Hiland, Ph.D.*
*President, Hiland Consulting*

# THE SUSTAINABLE HIGH ROI

## Fundraising System™

# THE SUSTAINABLE HIGH ROI

## Fundraising System™

JOANNE OPPELT, MHA

*The Sustainable High ROI Fundraising System*™

Published by Joanne Oppelt Consulting, LLC

Copyright © 2022 by Joanne Oppelt

Hardcover ISBN: 978-1-951978-24-2
Paperback ISBN: 978-1-951978-23-5
eBook ISBN: 978-1-951978-25-9

13 12 11 10 9 8 7 6 5 4 3 2 1

Printed in the United States of America

# Dedication

*This book is dedicated to my husband and children, who aided in my personal growth through my years of university studies and in staff positions—and who continue the tradition in my journey as a consultant. These four have helped me be a more empathetic and understanding mother, wife, and fundraising professional.*

# Table of Contents

# About the Author

During Joanne Oppelt's 30+ years working in the nonprofit arena, she has held positions from volunteer to executive director in both small and large organizations. Her extensive background puts her in a unique position to understand the challenges nonprofit leaders face—both internally and externally. As principal of Joanne Oppelt Consulting, LLC, she specializes in building fundraising programs with high returns on investment, helping local, regional, national, and international nonprofits raise more money, improve their ROI, increase net income, and realize continuous net surpluses.

The creator of *The Sustainable High ROI Fundraising System* and co-creator of the *Nonprofit Quick Guide* series, Joanne is the author of five books and coauthor of fourteen. She has taught at Kean University as an adjunct professor in its graduate program, and is also a highly sought-after speaker and presenter. She holds a master's degree in health administration from Wilkes University, where she graduated with distinction. Her bachelor's degree is in education, with a minor in psychology. She can be reached through her website at www.joanneoppeltcourses.com.

# Acknowledgements

First and foremost, I thank my husband, Rick. Without his support, I would never be an author. He is the one who has been by my side through the thick and thin of my fundraising career. I can never repay what he has given to me.

I am indebted to Mary Hiland, PhD, for our conversations and her manuscript review before publication. Mary's wisdom as a consultant and coach to executive directors and her knowledge of the field were invaluable. Thank you, Mary, for your patience and insight.

And to Christine Duncan, MSW, and Lucinda Mercer, CFRE, who also reviewed the book before publication. Your feedback resulted in a better book.

I would also like to thank my friend and colleague Stephen Nill, JD, who has pushed me into uncomfortable places where I grow. He has counseled me wisely and encouraged me along the way.

In addition, I owe a debt of gratitude to Cindy Schulson of Marketing with Heart, who taught me how to find the words that succinctly describe my fundraising system.

And, as always, there is a special place in my heart for all the nonprofit leaders with whom I have had the privilege to work. For it is through you that I have found professional fulfillment and satisfaction.

## Chapter One

# Inundated

So much to do, not enough time. So many financial and board pressures. You could use something that makes your life a little easier.

The Sustainable High ROI Fundraising System will do that, at least as far as fundraising is concerned. After implementing the system, you will work with board members who are engaged in fundraising. Your staff will meet your overall financial goals. Your community will monetarily support your cause. All by applying what is described in this book. Guaranteed, if you follow the principles outlined in the pages, you will spend less effort generating more net income than you dreamed possible.

## The Many Pressures of Executive Leadership

Where do you find the resources to get it all done? You're already working sixty to eighty hours a week, and there are still important tasks not being attended to. The revenue is never enough. The operational fires keep exploding. You can't find good fundraising staff. New donors aren't flocking to your agency. And your board remains disengaged in fundraising. What do you do?

You need a method to increase revenues in ways that will not increase your workload or give you one more thing to worry about. You need board and staff to work with you to raise money for your cause without demanding too much of your time. You want potential donors to come to you, eager and willing to give.

Implementing The Sustainable High ROI Fundraising System can help you. The system is specifically designed to:

- Build on your current efforts to lead the agency.

- Raise money in ways that don't tax, but build up, your organization's capacity.

- Create an infectious fundraising culture.

- Excite your community and raise your nonprofit's profile to draw people to your cause and financially support your organization.

- Leverage the never-enough resources available to you.

- Engage your board in fundraising.

- Reduce your stress.

- Give you more time to spend with friends and family.

## What Makes This Book Different?

Usually, fundraising books are about the mechanics of implementing specific fundraising activities such as writing appeal letters, asking for major gifts, writing grants, running capital campaigns, asking your board to fundraise, and the like. They tell you how to implement effective fundraising concepts, processes, and procedures. This book is different. This book will not tell you how to execute specific activities. It will, however, tell you how to implement a fundraising system that gets your board, staff, and community

### Clarifying Point

This book will not tell you how to execute specific activities. It will, however, tell you how to implement a fundraising system that gets your board, staff, and community excited about your mission, so they eagerly support it financially and recruit other donors to join them within the context of your current organizational capacity.

excited about your mission, so they eagerly support it financially and recruit other donors to join them. All within the context of your current organizational capacity. It will also tell you how to keep more of the money you raise.

This book is written for executive directors who want to raise more money to advance their nonprofit's missions. Based on my more than thirty years of nonprofit experience, this book teaches you specifically about The Sustainable High ROI Fundraising System and how you can use it to improve your fundraising program. The system does not change the individual elements that are part of fundraising, as they are what they are. Instead, it shows how they relate to each other and how they are all used to promote the mission.

So you can see how the system can be used in real life, I provide you with actual examples of how the system was applied to four nonprofits I have worked with. Just so you know, the examples are real, but some details have been changed to protect confidentiality.

In **Chapter Two**, I introduce you to The Sustainable High ROI Fundraising System, giving you a broad overview of the system and the context it operates in.

**Chapter Three** introduces four nonprofits we follow throughout the remainder of the book. I worked with these four nonprofits, implementing The Sustainable High ROI Fundraising System. You will see where they started in **Chapter Three** and whether or not they met their goals in **Chapter Eleven**.

**Chapter Four** describes the first step of the system, assessing your nonprofit's fundraising strengths and gaps. I explain what is included in a comprehensive evaluation, how to conduct a thorough assessment, and how this first step was applied to our four nonprofits.

**Chapter Five** talks about what you are evaluating. I cover the different types of giving, describing the most common fundraising methods. I also discuss the technology required to adequately track interactions with donors and their donations.

In **Chapter Six,** we move on to step two of the system and talk about how you can motivate and empower your board to fundraise.

Your goal is to empower your board to be mission ambassadors who teach your community how to interact with your agency.

**Chapter Seven** presents step three, describing how you can set your development staff up for fundraising success and meet your overall financial goals.

**Chapter Eight** discusses typical fundraising staff roles, including how to build your development department. We also talk about how to recruit, work with, and retain fundraising staff.

**Chapter Nine** covers how to build community awareness and backing so that the public supports your organization financially.

So that you can start customizing your fundraising program to meet the needs of your donors, **Chapter Ten** focuses on various groups of donors, their likes and preferences, and their motivations for giving.

In **Chapter Eleven**, we see how our four agencies fared after applying The Sustainable High ROI Fundraising System.

In **Chapter Twelve**, we wrap the book and tell you the next steps to take to move your own fundraising program forward.

By applying the system outlined in this book, you will:

- Acquire a solid foundation to build a highly successful fundraising program, shifting your fundraising focus from raising money to raising money *and* advancing the mission.

- Discover how to assess your nonprofit's fundraising strengths and weaknesses, empower and enthuse your board to fundraise, mobilize your staff for success in their fundraising endeavors, and excite your community to eagerly support your mission so that you enjoy continuous net surpluses.

- Learn how to create a robust fundraising organizational culture that stimulates your board, staff, and community to become consistent mission ambassadors for your nonprofit.

- See how to implement a fundraising system that raises more money at less cost, increasing your fundraising return on investment.

- Be confident you will raise the money you need to grow your agency and advance its mission.

## Bringing it Together

You deserve a financial break. You deserve staff and community support. You deserve quality time away from the office. Applying the strategies outlined in this book, you *will* achieve more net income to grow your agency and advance its mission with less effort than you realize. And that's the goal, isn't it? To efficiently and effectively facilitate more life-changing experiences to make the world better.

Good luck on your journey as you move forward in meeting your nonprofit's financial and mission goals!

## Points to Remember

- Recognizing you are inundated with overwhelming responsibilities, implementing The Sustainable High ROI Fundraising System can relieve the fundraising pressures of your job.

- The Sustainable High ROI Fundraising System will help you raise more revenues, allocate resources more efficiently, increase organizational capacity, attract new supporters, reduce your stress, and give you more time to spend with friends and family.

## What's Next?

Now that you know the benefits of implementing the system let's get a more detailed look at the system's components.

## Chapter Two

# System Relief

The Sustainable High ROI Fundraising System teaches you how to empower your board members to become mission leaders, facilitate fundraising staff success, and increase your return on fundraising investment by at least 100 percent.

## The Sustainable High ROI Fundraising System

Identifying your fundraising strengths and gaps

Empowering Your Board

Mobilizing Your Staff

Exciting Your Community

## What Makes This System Different?

Four key factors make my system unique:

1. I emphasize advancing mission just as much as raising money, so you build on your board's motivation for serving and increase your nonprofit's appeal to potential donors.

2. I don't just focus on raising revenues but also on ensuring your expenses are kept to a minimum to increase your return on investment.

3. I take a strategic approach that mobilizes all your stakeholders—your board, staff, *and* community.

4. I help you create a culture shift within your nonprofit so that board members and staff become consistent mission ambassadors for your organization.

## The Results You Can Achieve

Using this system gives your nonprofit more financial reserves, money to improve infrastructure, and funds to build long-term financial assets. The idea is to solidify your nonprofit's financial position and allow your agency to grow its impact and advance its mission. Specifically, you will have:

- Immediate ways to raise more money
- Staff and board working together in their respective roles
- Increasingly larger donations
- More awareness of your nonprofit
- Increased community support
- More donors
- Reduced overall fundraising costs
- Ongoing net surpluses

Using this system raises more money while expending fewer organizational resources for a higher return on your fundraising investment. And, because you build on your nonprofit's unique strengths, you create a custom fundraising program that leverages existing fundraising assets, which you can easily adapt to changing conditions.

## Putting the System into Context

Assessing your fundraising strengths and gaps, empowering your board, mobilizing your staff, and exciting your community can seem overwhelming.

### Clarifying Point

In any one day, a nonprofit executive director's duties can include:

- Managing operations
- Satisfying funders and donors
- Informing and inspiring board, staff, and volunteers
- Listening to clients
- Communicating your mission and accomplishments to the public
- Assessing community needs
- Collaborating with community agencies
- Raising money
- Reviewing (and worrying about) finances
- Keeping the agency afloat
- Growing the agency
- Managing facilities
- Solving technology problems
- Studying and implementing proper human resource regulations and policies
- Cleaning the office
- Unjamming the copier
- Whatever else decides to rear its ugly head

How do you prioritize fundraising and still get it all done? Where do you find time in the day to raise the money to keep the agency afloat, much less grow it? How do you juggle the overwhelming task of fundraising with managing the day-to-day operations of service delivery?

The answer is to leverage what you and your staff are already doing, with your fundraising centered on mission attainment, not raising dollars.

## Take Time to Breathe

Take a deep breath and hold it in for ten seconds. Slowly exhale. Take another deep breath and hold it. Slowly exhale again. Keep breathing deeply while you ponder. You've got this.

Then look at what you're already doing to fundraise, which is inherent in everything you do. Supervising operations, including managing facilities, solving technology problems, and implementing good human resource practices, is crucial to successfully delivering services. In other words, overseeing operations is overseeing your mission in action, which is what fundraising is about. Collaborating with other community agencies leverages your agency's resources to increase mission fulfillment, donations, and net income. Knowing your community's needs helps you craft your case for support to donors. Thoughtful and deliberate public relations practices create greater community awareness and lead to expanded community support. Sound financial management makes sure there is enough money to support it all.

> ### Encouragement
>
> You've got this. You're already doing a lot of what fundraising is about.

## Focus on Your Mission

As overseeing operations is about your nonprofit's mission in action, you should infuse mission into your fundraising activities. Fundraising is not about money. You are not developing relationships with donors with the intent to raise money. You are raising money to meet community needs as expressed in your agency's mission statement. Fundraising is about showing potential donors how they make an impact on a cause they care about. It is the mission, not money, that motivates people to give.

Be careful about accepting gifts that are only tangentially related to your mission. And always do your research to make sure it is ethical for you to receive the gift. Be judicious in what funding you accept. You don't want to end up running programs that have little to do with or are in conflict with your mission. Avoid even a little mission drift. I have seen it ruin more than one nonprofit.

### Individual Donations

Individual donors give to nonprofits through direct donations, peer-to-peer campaigns, tickets to special events, and auctions and raffles held at those events. You are hoping to raise money through them. In the case of direct donations, your donors' goal is to make an impact on a cause they believe in. In the case of peer-to-peer campaigns, they want to support their friends or family. In the case of event attendance, they want to have a nice day or evening out with some of the money going to a good cause. Although all these methods will raise some money, which will raise the most money *and* promote your mission? Because you want to promote your mission above all else.

And here's why. It so happens that individual donations, particularly email campaigns and large personal gifts, cost less to realize than other forms of fundraising. In addition to costing the least to raise, repeat individual donors tend to give for long periods. They are a more stable source of funding than grants that have to be applied for every year, government contracts that have onerous reporting requirements and must be renewed annually, and special events that are labor-intensive and raise money at a single point in time. Peer-to-peer campaigns have the advantage that someone else raises the money with your nonprofit as the beneficiary. Special events are fun and can bring a community together.

If your agency engages in these types of fundraising activities, they need to be mission-related for two primary reasons. Number one, your agency's mission is what motivates individuals to give. Individual donors are interested in impacting a problem they care about. And the issue is expressed through your mission. Number two, your mission centralizes your message. You want your community to know exactly what your organization does and what it stands for. Which means your nonprofit must communicate strong, consistent messages. And consistent messages are communicated through word and deed; in other words, they encompass everything the organization says and does. That is why you want your fundraising related to your mission. So you leverage your fundraising efforts with what you are already doing as an organization.

### Foundation Funding

Lack of funding is not a need for foundations. Like individuals, foundations are interested in solving community issues they care about. To get the grant funding, you need to ask for help in making a significant impact on your community instead of asking for money. And the issue that your nonprofit addresses is memorialized in its mission statement. To get foundation funding, you match missions—the issues they care about to the issues your agency addresses. It's all about the mission.

> **Words of Wisdom**
>
> Always put the mission first. Always.

### Corporate Giving

When you pursue business donations, it is also essential to keep the mission front and center. Because businesses are interested in partnering with nonprofits with good brands and mission fulfillment is the crux of your nonprofit's brand.

### Government Contracts

Government funders, too, are interested in mission impact. The government ostensibly provides funding to fix community problems. And your mission states the community issue your nonprofit effects. To get government funding, match your agency's mission to the purpose of the legislation.

## Engage in Strategic Planning

Creating or updating your nonprofit's strategic plan should be done before implementing The Sustainable High ROI Fundraising System.

You must assess where your nonprofit is today and set goals for its future to move forward. And then you need to define the specific actions that will reach those goals. That means engaging in strategic planning. The Sustainable High ROI Fundraising System does not operate in a vacuum. It engages the board, staff, and community. To keep them all on the same page, have an up-to-date strategic plan.

And then don't let that plan sit on a shelf. Use it as your blueprint. Using your strategic plan as a guide, you can inform the board, staff, and volunteers of your progress, create excitement around mission fulfillment, and get your board, staff, volunteers, and donors excited about contributing. It is the mission that motivates. If you can measure and communicate progress in fulfilling your organization's mission, which a thoughtfully developed strategic plan can help you do, you've taken a huge first step toward meeting your fundraising goals.

## Prioritize Long-Term Goals

Once you have a strategic plan in place, structure your workload to meet *both* your short-term and long-term goals. We are so busy putting out fires. We put out fires every day. But you can't spend all your time putting out fires. You need water to put out the fires. You need time to build the pipeline for getting the water. And then you need to get the water. Have you tried letting someone else deal with the fire so you can expand your access to water?

In other words, can you delegate the immediate task to someone else so that you have time to get into the crux of The Sustainable High ROI Fundraising System, that is, nurturing relationships with your board, staff, and community? Who else can deal with the issue of the day while you're creating the environment for successful fundraising and building necessary funding relationships? The point is, you must prioritize getting those long-term objectives addressed. Who does exactly what is a matter of how big your staff is and who has what strengths and weaknesses. As an executive director, you can delegate many tasks. What you can't delegate is getting out there and building the foundational relationships that will lead to greater mission fulfillment and funding.

As an executive director of a small agency, I spent 70 percent of my week on day-to-day operations and 30 percent building foundational relationships. What I found is captured in these three statements:

1. When equipped with the proper tools and given the opportunity, my staff rose to the occasion.

2. My expectations about what I could do needed to be realistic.

3. I wasn't as indispensable as I thought.

The benefits of stepping back for 30 percent of the time far exceeded what I hoped.

## Delegate to Others

Increased mission fulfillment led to increased funding. When I challenged my staff to reach new heights, they became more engaged in their work. The greater engagement in their work led to greater productivity which, in turn, led to increased mission fulfillment. Which led to increased funding. An upward cycle of obtaining funding to better fulfill the mission had begun.

My staff also felt more empowered and appreciated because I believed in them. Of course, they needed the proper tools to meet their responsibilities, which I could provide because I was spending 30 percent of my time meeting long-term fundraising goals and garnering resources. Feeling more appreciated and empowered by me resulted in their greater job satisfaction which, in turn, led to further engagement, which reduced my employee retention costs. My nonprofit's net income improved. Voila! Increased fundraising revenues by delegating to others.

## Set Realistic Expectations

Change is always slower than we want it to be. Development is called development for a reason: it takes time to build strong and lasting relationships. Sometimes you need to sacrifice short-term results for long-term sustainability. Successful change is achieved more little by little than in one fell swoop. Once you and your board understand this and expectations are more realistic, relationships will improve. Which means board members have good experiences and feel better about being involved with the agency. And, since there is less conflict at the board level, there is more time to talk about the strategic partnerships you and the board need to form to implement The Sustainable High ROI Fundraising System. The intervention happens over months, not days or weeks. Be patient with yourself and give yourself time to develop the relationships you need to show significant results.

## Take Care of Yourself

Once I realized I didn't have to do it all and delegated more, board relations improved. I relaxed a little. Since I wasn't feeling pressured (mainly by me) to meet unrealistic expectations, had others helping me put out fires, and was increasing net income, I could get away for a couple of hours. Or a day. Or even a whole week. I could take time to engage in self-care activities. I could rejuvenate. Which is extremely important for an executive director to do. As an executive director, you set the tone for your agency. A more positive, refreshed, relaxed environment will make for positive experiences both in the office and the boardroom. Positive staff and board experiences improve overall agency morale. Happier staff and board members communicate more positively with volunteers and donors. Repeated positive interactions with contributors lead to greater engagement. Greater volunteer and donor engagement translate into higher contributions and improved donor and volunteer retention. Which results in better fundraising results.

## Bringing It Together

As an executive director, you are responsible for the success of your agency. So much demands your attention. And finances are a constant worry. It is imperative that you meet your agency's financial obligations and grow your mission.

Remember, you are interested in raising money. Your donors aren't, though. Donors are interested in mission impact. Clearly communicate what your nonprofit stands for through everything it says and does.

Leverage your fundraising activities with your communications. And watch for mission drift. No matter the funding channel— individuals, foundations, businesses, or government—a mission emphasis will always produce the best results.

Good strategic planning, prioritizing long-term goals, delegating to others, setting realistic expectations, and engaging in self-care lead to increased mission fulfillment, better board relations, greater productivity, increased donations, and reduced costs. Which, in turn, positively impact your nonprofit's bottom line. By planning, delegating, taking care of yourself, and chipping away at your long-term goals, your agency can see incredible increases in donations and net income.

Using the framework for the system, you will focus on the mission rather than the money. You will attract more people to your cause. Good strategic planning keeps the board and staff on the same page. Setting targets and showing your progress in reaching them motivates your board and staff to move forward while showing the community that exciting things are happening at your nonprofit. I survived by setting realistic goals, involving others, and taking care of myself—the hardest part.

No, it wasn't easy. Yes, it did take time. No, I didn't always feel qualified for the job. We did it, though. With less board tension, a more challenged and engaged staff, a slow but steady pace forward, and a rejuvenated me, I had the energy to assess our organization's fundraising strengths and gaps, empower my board, mobilize my staff, and excite my community. Then our fundraising results drastically improved. And we achieved our financial goals. We had more resources to help us meet and grow our mission.

## Points to Remember

- Fundraising is about fulfilling the mission, not raising money. Individual, foundation, business, and government funders are all interested in mission identity and attainment.

- Keep your nonprofit's mission focus strong. Be judicious in what gifts you accept. The last thing you want is for your mission to drift off course.

- As you move to implement the system, take time to breathe, engage in strategic planning, prioritize long-term goals, delegate to others, set realistic expectations, and take care of yourself.

## What's Next?

In the next chapter, we begin our exploration of four nonprofits that came to me with diverse fundraising goals, infrastructures, levels of board leadership, and staff capacities. They were quite different from each other, but all wanted to raise more money.

## Chapter Three

# What a State of Affairs

I n this chapter, you are introduced to four very different nonprofits and what they wanted to do regarding their fundraising programs.

## Regional First Responder Assistance Agency

This nonprofit had a mission to support area first responder units in obtaining needed equipment and volunteers. It wanted to do three things: acquire younger donors to increase fundraising revenues, become more visible by becoming a volunteer center, and develop volunteer leaders for succession planning purposes. It was ahead of the game in terms of succession planning—most nonprofits don't consider succession planning until they are faced with an unexpected resignation or life circumstance that results in a key person's absence.

It had existed for about sixty years. Its annual budget was around $2 million, of which it gave $1.6 million in grants to area police, firefighter, and EMT units. And it did it only through individual donations. It enjoyed a strong financial position of twenty-four months of operating reserves. And it wanted to keep it that way.

Its small part-time staff of five supported about one hundred volunteers who led and did the agency's fundraising, volunteer recruitment, and grant allocation work. It had a board of fifteen members and was happy with that size. It was also happy with its board structure. In addition to the executive committee, it had volunteer recruitment, program, fundraising, finance, audit, and marketing committees. Except for the executive committee, its committees included community volunteers as well as board members. Once agreeing to serve, most volunteers stayed for many years and moved up the leadership ladder. As a result, the organization was well-connected to the community and its leaders.

Its donor base was pretty loyal, evident through a high overall donor retention rate. One hundred percent of its board gave an annual major gift each year. Many of its donors were also major givers. The problem was that as its older donors retired, moved away, or passed on, it had not been able to replace them.

The agency was in the early stages of developing a corporate giving program. It had good relationships with area businesses but had never asked them for money.

Its software was a significant obstacle to donor growth. Its donor-tracking system was outdated and couldn't easily accommodate efficiencies in recording and reporting on recurring gifts. It also didn't have the capabilities to easily personalize appeals with previous donation data.

To build on its existing donor base, it needed a way to encourage increased giving for current donors. It needed a communications strategy to reach younger donors and future leaders. It needed to leverage its recent business outreach with a corporate fundraising program. It needed to structure fundraising activities to avoid further stretching organizational capacity. And It needed a new low-cost fundraising software solution that could more efficiently process donations, keep better records, and generate more-detailed reports.

On the other hand, I saw several strengths: strong financial management and reporting systems, focus on individual giving, strong volunteer structure and dedicated volunteers, and previous contact with the business community.

I needed to get a comprehensive understanding of what was going on and confirm my perceptions. So the next step was to thoroughly assess its fundraising strengths and gaps. (I cover how we tackled that in the next chapter.)

## Statewide Domestic Violence Transitional Housing Agency

This nonprofit provided transitional housing to women and their children fleeing their abusers. Residents could stay for up to eighteen months while participating in psychological counseling, receiving job training, securing employment, and locating permanent housing. The agency was clear and focused on what it wanted to do with me: increase foundation and corporate support. It already had a pretty good funding mix with government grants, fees for service, special events, a small number of individual donations, a small amount of investment income, and rental income. With an already good diversity of funding sources, the organization hired me to cover all its fundraising bases.

Its twenty-five-year history was one of financial growth. It had started with one government service contract covering two direct service staff members at $200,000 over two years. It now boasted twenty-five supportive housing properties across the state and added one or two each year. With an annual budget of around $30 million, it employed about 550 full- and part-time staff members, two in its development department. Its financial position was enviably strong with continuous positive net income, six months of operating reserves, and considerable long-term assets in the form of properties it owned.

It was also growing in terms of mission impact. Its board of nine included three clients that the nonprofit served. As a result, the board retained a solid understanding of and dedication to the agency's mission. That understanding filtered down through the staff, who, as a group, were also extraordinarily mission-driven.

Because government grants were essential to funding service delivery and acquiring new properties, it effectively nurtured its political connections. It enjoyed excellent relationships with both legislators and government staff. It also had event fundraising down to a science, hosting four major fundraising events each year with high client participation. It was important to the organization that it be as inclusive as possible.

Not all was rosy, however. It lacked community visibility outside its field, departments were pretty siloed, and it exhibited little foundation expertise. And its fundraising relationships with businesses did not extend beyond sponsorships of its events.

To meet its goals of increased foundation and corporate funding, this organization needed a way to get its staff working together to fundraise, a way to reach the broader community, a foundation funding plan, more ways for businesses to be involved with them, and corporate donor recruitment and retention plans.

It needed to create effective and efficient foundation and corporate giving programs. So the next step was to thoroughly assess its fundraising strengths and gaps. The goal was to build on its strengths and compensate for the weaknesses. How we tackled that is covered in **Chapter Four**.

## Community Drug Prevention Agency

This nonprofit, with a mission to prevent substance abuse through education aimed at high-risk youth, was in trouble. It was experiencing declining support from donors, including foundation and event support. Its financial reserves were gone, and its funders were starting to question its financial viability. To survive, it needed to increase revenues, build up financial reserves, and improve its reputation in the community.

This nonprofit realized low operational expenses with a volunteer service delivery system and only employed a full-time executive director and six part-time staff. Its annual budget was around $600,000. It had been in existence for about fifteen years and was governed by a board of twelve. Its recordkeeping systems had suffered over the years and were a mess by the time I got involved.

Its defining attribute was the dedication to the mission by the board, staff, volunteers, donors, vendors, advocates, and the community. Everyone, and I mean everyone, who had anything to do with this agency was highly dedicated to mission fulfillment. Its level of dedication to the mission is the highest I've encountered. However, aside from the executive director, the board and volunteers were unwilling to fundraise.

To support its delivery system, the organization had volunteer recruitment, training, development, and recognition down pat. Whatever I was going to do for it, I would build on its strong volunteer base. My initial assessment was it needed to improve recordkeeping systems, secure low-cost fundraising software, develop a profitable fundraising plan, repair its reputation, get more people fundraising, and foster board fundraising leadership.

Our first task was to fully understand the details behind the decline and how we could turn the obvious negatives into positives. So, we started assessing its fundraising strengths and gaps in detail. I will discuss how in the next chapter.

## International Maternal Health Education Agency

With a mission to prevent low birth weight in the world's poorest countries and a history of only four years, this nonprofit needed to increase general operating revenues. It also wanted more board engagement in fundraising and guidance in setting up a fundraising team.

It had grown quickly. Its annual budget was now about $6 million, having doubled over the last two years. It was on an upward growth trajectory, accompanied by the problem of resource acquisition not keeping up with demand for services. Its dedicated staff and board of five were stretched to the limit. It had more work than it could handle. Its evidence-based programs and practices were well received by the international community.

Its funding was 80 percent from various government entities, about 20 percent from foundations and a small number of individual donations. The staff was excellent in applying for, getting, and keeping government funding. It was not so good at reaching individual donors. It did not have 100 percent board giving. It had no donor recruitment or retention plans, major gift programs, or planned giving vehicles. Because of the international dispersion of its programming, it was not interested in hosting fundraising events. It was, however, interested in developing a business giving program.

Because programming had grown so fast, there was minimal fundraising infrastructure. The program-focused staff had never been exposed to fundraising. They tracked their governmental funding on excel spreadsheets. There was no fundraising recordkeeping except for that. They also needed new messaging, as what they currently had did not reflect all the recent changes in the organization.

Clearly, this nonprofit needed to introduce fundraising into its organizational culture. It needed individual and business giving programs that would not tax staff any further than they were already. It also needed a low-maintenance donor software solution and a fundraising staffing plan that could grow with them.

## Bringing It Together

As you can see, these four nonprofits were different from one another. They had diverse missions, geographical scopes, organizational capacities, ages, stages in the life cycle, budgets, financial positions, funding streams, levels of expertise in fundraising, levels of board involvement in fundraising, levels of staff involvement in fundraising, levels of volunteer development and involvement, and community outreach infrastructures. Clearly, they would need unique, customized interventions to reach their desired outcomes.

There were many similarities, though. I find these similarities indicative of the nonprofit arena. They all exhibited dedication to their missions. They all wanted more general operating funds. Each of them wanted to acquire new donors. They all needed to integrate fundraising with other organizational systems, be it program, finance, marketing, communications, or IT. All needed robust recordkeeping and reporting systems, better outreach to the community, and messaging to raise their visibility.

After the initial conversations, the first steps were to conduct complete and thorough assessments of their fundraising strengths and gaps. That way we could develop interventions to capitalize on their strengths and work efficiently within their unique missions, communities, and organizational capacities.

## Points to Remember

- Nonprofits come in all shapes and sizes with individualized fundraising goals, infrastructure, board leadership, and staff capacities. For best results, you want to create a fundraising intervention customized to your nonprofit's unique characteristics.

- Many fundraising issues are consistent throughout the nonprofit world, including dedication to mission, need for general operating funds, integrated fundraising systems, community visibility and outreach, and strong messaging.

- The first step to improving fundraising results starts with a complete and thorough assessment of your fundraising strengths and gaps.

## What's Next?

Just what is a thorough assessment of your fundraising strengths and gaps? How comprehensive should the assessment be? Who should conduct it? What do you do with the results? We answer these questions in the next chapter.

## Chapter Four

# Assessing Your Fundraising Strengths and Gaps

F or the best financial results, you need to assess the efficiency and effectiveness of your agency's fundraising strategy and use of organizational mission and financial assets. You take a strengths-based approach, laying the basis for choosing effective ways to raise money that will work within the parameters of your nonprofit's capacity while at the same time growing it. As a result, you can create a customized action plan to move your fundraising forward and establish benchmarks for measuring progress. This chapter explains how a thorough assessment and thoughtful plan lead to better fundraising results; lists the mission, financial, and fundraising components you measure; and gives direction on conducting the evaluation.

Results you can expect after implementing this step:

- a financial strategy that leverages your agency's fundraising assets and works within your organization's capacity;

- an action plan that shows you how to take the next step toward financial stability and mission impact; and

- improvement in your fundraising return on investment by at least 100 percent.

## Executing a Complete and Thorough Assessment

To formulate successful fundraising plans, you need to research and truly understand all the ways your nonprofit is unique. That means conducting a complete and thorough fundraising assessment. And by complete, I don't just mean evaluating your development department's fundraising implementation and financial performance. No. By complete, I mean thoroughly assessing all parts of your agency that influence fundraising and impact your development department's ability to raise money. Like board giving and fundraising leadership. And software adequacy. And marketing infrastructure and implementation. And volunteer recruitment and development.

Thorough also means gathering data at both the macro and micro levels. You want overall organizational data as well as individual unit data. You want to be able to spot significant trends and have the details on which to analyze the causes of your findings.

Essential things to assess include:

- Board fundraising structure and leadership
- Organizational fundraising savvy and readiness
- Overall agency financial performance and trends
- Strategic plans and processes
- Development plans and processes
- Marketing plans and processes
- Communication plans and processes
- Donation policies and processes
- Target group research activities and processes
- Gift statistics
- Donor profile
- Donor statistics
- Donor prospecting activities and processes
- Donor cultivation activities and processes
- Donor stewardship activities and processes

- Fundraising performance
  - Overall
  - By fundraising channel
  - By individual fundraising activity
  - Trends
- Fundraising recordkeeping and reporting software
- Fundraising volunteer recruitment, development, and recognition activities processes and activities

As you can see, this is quite a list. You may find you want to contract the assessment out since collecting and analyzing all this data may overtax your staff, leading to low morale and burnout. If that happens, your fundraising will really suffer. Plus, an objective person who has worked with multiple nonprofits can better see where the organizational gaps are, assure you that your nonprofit is not alone, and offer more solutions to whatever the assessment shows.

You can, however, collect and analyze data in-house. Just be prepared to allocate weeks of staff time toward the effort. And run the numbers, accounting for staff time and what you won't do because the staff is working on this. You may find that hiring a consultant is less expensive than what you lose in staff time and opportunity costs.

## Who Assesses What, When?

Different people are responsible for different areas of the organization. You, as executive director, of course, have overall responsibility for the functioning of the agency. The board has a duty to make sure that resources are used to meet the mission, not personal benefit. Staff have operational data. As such, different people in different roles will tackle different parts of the assessment, either because a consultant has asked them for the information or the agency is undergoing its own thorough evaluation. And, to use time efficiently and not stress organizational capacity, different parts of the assessment need to be monitored and reevaluated at different times.

## Who?

When you undergo your assessment, appoint one person to be the repository for all the collected information. You want a central place for information retrieval. And, although many people will contribute, you want only one person to write the evaluation report so that it is in one voice and easy to read. That person is usually a consultant or senior development staff person.

You will also need working groups to collect information, coordinate staff and community feedback, and interpret the data. The board and executive director will give input regarding board matters. The executive director and chief financial officer will give input regarding agency finances. The executive director and senior development staff person will give input regarding the fundraising performance. The senior development staff person and senior marketing or communications staff person will give input relating to all things marketing and communications. The senior development staff person and senior IT staff person will have input in technology requirements. The senior development staff person and senior volunteer staff person may give feedback regarding fundraising volunteers.

## When?

You should also think about who will monitor the information and how often it will be evaluated: daily, weekly, monthly, quarterly, semiannually, annually, biannually, or longer. And reevaluate things whenever a significant change has occurred, such as a change in executive leadership or your external environment, a reorganization, or a merger.

For example, as an executive director, I monitored finances and analyzed them almost daily. I looked at progress toward the goals in our strategic plan monthly. I brought out my communications plan semiannually. Whatever *your* schedule, just make sure you review data as often as you need to meet your daily, monthly, quarterly, semiannual, and annual goals.

## Getting the Most from Your Assessment

Once you complete the assessment of your fundraising strengths and gaps, take the findings, analyze them, and develop a customized fundraising strategy that leverages your agency's uniqueness and works within your organization's capacity. Take your strategy and create an action plan. In addition to development staff, get input from all organizational units that affect and support fundraising processes and results, including finance, marketing, communications, program, and governance. The action plan will help you implement progressive steps toward the financial stability and mission impact you desire. By implementing your action plan based on the concepts we discuss in **Chapters Six, Seven**, and **Nine**, you will see an improvement in your fundraising return on investment of at least 100 percent.

## Fundraising Plans: One Size Does NOT Fit All

Once you have all the data from your assessment, you can create a customized fundraising plan that truly addresses all the ways your nonprofit is unique. I have been asked to implement a particular fundraising activity several times throughout my career because Organization X raised hundreds of thousands of dollars by doing it. While I, too, want to raise hundreds of thousands of dollars, I do not want to do it solely based on what worked for someone else. I will research the activity to see if it will work for the agency I'm working with, but even if it does, I will make modifications.

Every nonprofit is unique. Its unique qualities must be accounted for to be successful at raising the big bucks. For example, I have worked with nonprofits

### Clarifying Point

A thorough fundraising assessment will account for your specific mission, community makeup, organizational capacity, and stage in the life cycle, including evaluating board structure and leadership, organizational readiness, overall financial performance, fundraising policies and procedures, planning systems, research systems, and recordkeeping and reporting systems.

that are successful at raising money through walk-a-thons. And I have worked with nonprofits who tried to emulate that success and failed miserably, losing money on the event. Truly, every nonprofit is different. And those differences must be factored into your fundraising activities if you plan on fundraising success.

## Accounting for Differences in Mission

One of the differences lies in your nonprofit's mission. Few nonprofits struggling to raise funds align their fundraising activities to promote their mission. If you want to successfully engage people with your nonprofit, you need to continuously promote your mission. Money follows mission.

## Accounting for Differences in Community Makeup

Another difference lies in your community's makeup. To reach new donors, you need to define who your community is, that is, the people that you want to reach. And "anyone who has money to donate" is not an acceptable answer. You need to target your communications to specific groups so they will listen to you, addressing their precise needs through the exact communication channels they prefer with references to their distinct values and beliefs.

Most nonprofits just don't have the capacity to do that for too many target groups. Be specific. Narrowly target who you want to reach. You will end up with not as many prospects but more prospects who are ready to give. We talk more about exciting your community in **Chapter Nine**.

## Accounting for Different Organizational Capacities

Different organizational capacities also dictate the type of fundraising activities in which your nonprofit should invest. Even if it has the same mission, each organization has its own unique strengths and weaknesses. Board and staff expertise may differ. They may be different in size. Or they may be in different financial positions. All of these things affect organizational capacity. It's essential to account for your nonprofit's unique organizational capacity to carry out the fundraising activities you are considering and not pursue them just because some other agency found them effective or everyone likes the idea.

Run the numbers, including the labor involved, to see if you really get ahead by doing them. And account for other costs, too, like the effect on volunteer and staff morale. As well as the opportunity costs of not doing something else. You'll realize the best results by leveraging, instead of taxing, your resources.

## Accounting for Differences Over the Life Cycle

Different organizations may also be in different stages of their life cycles. Your mix of fundraising activities will be more diverse when you are just starting out than in ten years. In ten years, your board, staff, and volunteers will be more developed and experienced. Your organizational goals will be different, including your revenue goals. You will have slightly different reasons for raising money, which is a sign it is time to evaluate your current fundraising plans, goals, and objectives and revise them as necessary. You want them to fit into your new reality.

Don't just keep doing a fundraising element because it has worked in the past. What worked in the past worked in the past. If you have a new reality—if your nonprofit has grown and changed over the years—you have a different present. Make sure you assess whether your continuing fundraising activities still fit your present situation.

# How It Worked in Real Life

So, what does this look like in real life? How did the four agencies, highlighted in **Chapter Three,** tackle their assessments?

## Regional First Responder Assistance Agency

The executive director was my point of contact for this agency. I gave the executive director a questionnaire, including questions about mission and mission growth, board leadership and structure, financial health and performance, fundraising infrastructure, marketing and communications endeavors, and volunteer recruitment, training, and development systems. She completed the form in partnership with her board executive committee. I received the information, analyzed the data, and reported back to the executive director. The executive director took the information to her board and volunteer programming committee. The programming committee prioritized what to work on first, second, third, and so on. The executive director and I then discussed the scope of the rest of my contract and we went to work.

What was notable in this nonprofit was the depth of the relationships with community government and leadership. This was a strength we definitely wanted to build on in recruiting new individual donors. They also had a basic donation infrastructure, including having defined major gift levels and created corresponding materials. We needed to focus on developing a process for moving individual donors up the donor ladder. The existing volunteer structure was robust and worked well for them. We would incorporate fundraising into the existing structure too, starting with the board. The agency could then incorporate fundraising expectations into their volunteer recruitment, training, and leadership development standards and materials.

## Statewide Domestic Violence Transitional Housing Agency

I worked with the development director at this agency. The development director and I fashioned a questionnaire that we could get staff to answer given their limited time. The development director worked with the executive director to get the board's perspective. I received the information and analyzed it. I then met with the development director to talk about my findings, who prepared a report for the executive director for his approval. The executive director prioritized the work to be done. I then worked with the development director to craft a foundation and business fundraising plan to meet the agency's fundraising goals.

In conducting its assessment, I found that this organization, a mature agency, already had a solid mission-focused culture and board and staff infrastructures in place. And it wasn't interested in changing them. The executive director was the one who interacted directly with the board, so the development director and I needed to use nontraditional means to get the board involved in fundraising. Since departments were pretty siloed, another issue was that we needed a way to get staff working together on fundraising. This meant infusing fundraising into the organizational culture. As a large agency, it had many businesses it interacted with on many levels. We could use these relationships to initiate a business giving program. We would build its foundation program through research and staff training, highlighting the differences between foundation and government requests for funding and reporting requirements.

## Community Drug Prevention Agency

At this agency, I worked with the executive director, staff, and board. I administered the board and staff surveys, coordinated the feedback, and reported back to the executive director. The executive director then had me present to the board. The board prioritized what they wanted to be done. I discussed organizational capacity with the executive director, and together, we outlined a plan to meet the board's goals.

The assessment of this nonprofit confirmed my perceptions of what needed to be done: reputation repair, a swift influx of cash, training in what fundraising was and wasn't, more people fundraising for them, and board leadership in fundraising. The assessment also revealed the extent to which the organizational recordkeeping systems had deteriorated and that no one really knew how dire finances were. We would need this agency to develop a plan to correct its weaknesses, share it with important donors, implement fundraising activities that produced almost immediate results, get its recordkeeping systems in order, and work with the board to develop fundraising leadership.

## International Maternal Health Education Agency

This agency was in the middle of an executive director search. Three executive staff helped get board input and assisted me in conducting a comprehensive SWOT analysis.

The results of their assessment surprised them. They had many strengths on which to build a fundraising structure that would yield more general operating monies, including the existing program research protocols and financial reporting systems, collaborative culture, appetitive for excellence, and overwhelming desire to change their current situation. Caught up in the day-to-day operational issues that arose, they could only see the weaknesses of their position; it was eye-opening to see such strength.

That revelation laid the basis for developing a robust fundraising structure that would yield the increased unrestricted funding they wanted. As they had almost no fundraising infrastructure in place, it was invigorating to work from the ground up.

I then prioritized what needed to be done, put a timeline to it, and brought it to the group for their feedback. The group talked it over and determined the final scope of activities and their timing. We then moved to the second stage of the engagement, which I report on in **Chapter Six**.

## Bringing It Together

Do a thorough assessment, including all organizational units that interact with resource development in any way. Don't leave it to only one person. Even a consultant will work with different people in your organization to get all the information they need. Different people in different roles will have access to certain information and more expertise in one area than others. When you assess, you need a lead person to keep the information and write the reports to be in one voice.

Regularly assess your situation and progress in meeting your goals. Some areas are best assessed daily. Some monthly, some quarterly, some annually, and some biannually. Just make sure you regularly evaluate. Especially when there are changes in circumstances.

Use your assessment results to implement fundraising activities that engage people in your mission and leverage your strengths. Base plans on present conditions, not past ones. Take the time to regularly evaluate your plans to see if they are still the best option, given your current circumstances. Do what *your* nonprofit, not someone else's, needs to do to raise the most money you can.

One fundraising plan does not fit all nonprofits, even nonprofits in the same community with similar missions, sizes, or budgets. Each nonprofit is different. And your agency's uniqueness must be reflected in your fundraising plans for you to realize the most from whatever fundraising activities you choose to implement.

## Points to Remember

- To make modifications to general fundraising ideas, begin by assessing your nonprofit's fundraising strengths and gaps. Do a complete and thorough assessment, including board leadership, infrastructure and performance, financial health, marketing and communications endeavors, and volunteer recruitment and development as they relate to raising money.

- Although many people will gather and analyze data, appoint one person to be the keeper of the data and author findings.

- Regularly monitor and evaluate results. Always conduct an assessment whenever the agency undergoes a significant shift such as a change in executive directors, a major happening in the community, a reorganization, or a merger.

- For best results, tailor your fundraising plans to your nonprofit's unique characteristics. Make sure what you are designing accounts for your organization's particular mission, community, donor base, budget, and organizational capacity.

## What's Next?

So, you want to assess your fundraising strengths and gaps and create an action plan to move your fundraising efforts forward. What revenue-generating options do you have to choose from? What types of gift-giving are typical? For answers, see the next chapter.

## Chapter Five

# Let Me Count the Ways

To thoroughly assess your nonprofit's strengths and gaps and complete step one of The Sustainable High ROI Fundraising System, you need to understand the types of gift-giving you are inventorying. This chapter covers the most common types of fundraising activities that make up most fundraising systems and the technology you need to track the donations you receive.

There are many ways to raise money. Knowing what they are allows you to make decisions about how you will generate fundraising revenue. Your board is probably unaware of all the fundraising vehicles for gift-giving. Most board members only have knowledge of grants and special events as ways to raise money. And that's okay; they don't need to know all the details of every single way to raise money. They need to know enough to understand why the allocations in the budget for fundraising are what they are. This doesn't mean giving them a treatise on all the different ways to fundraise. It does mean that you should be able to speak to return on investment and cost to raise a dollar as the basis for your decision-making. Chances are, it will be an eye-opener for your board.

## Types of Fundraising

Money is given to nonprofits by individuals, foundations, businesses, and the government. (Fundraising events, by the way, are often a hybrid of individual and business giving.)

Donors donate through various fundraising techniques. Development professionals plan and execute donation pages, direct mail campaigns, phone-a-thons, text-to-give messaging, crowdfunding and peer-to-peer campaigns, major gift campaigns, major and planned giving programs, and capital campaigns, to name the most common. They also approach donors through donor-advised funds. To garner monies from foundations and the government, they write and submit proposals. To realize gifts from businesses, they ask for monetary and in-kind donations, submit proposals, create sponsored events, and develop employee volunteer opportunities. We go into detail about these techniques in the following pages.

The costs to raise one dollar varies by the type of activity. Here are the average costs:

- $0.10 through major gifts and capital campaigns, including labor
- $0.20 through grant writing, including labor
- $0.25 through direct mail renewal with a 50 percent or higher return rate, including labor
- $0.25 through planned giving, including labor
- $0.50 through fundraising events, *not* including labor
- $1.50 through direct mail acquisition with a 1 percent or higher return rate, including labor

### Clarifying Point

Your return on investment will vary according to the fundraising method you implement.

When choosing what fundraising methods to employ, remember your costs. Your return on investment will vary according to the fundraising method.

## Individual Giving

People engage with nonprofits by giving money, donating goods or services, or volunteering. Donors give equally by cash and online. Other individual-giving channels include in-kind donations, membership fees, voice calls, text messaging, donor-advised funds, and bequests, among others.

According to data from Charitable Giving in the USA of 2019, produced by CAF America, the median individual donation is around $100 while the mean is around $460. Individual donors are more likely to give if their contributions are matched. People increase their gifts because they have more money themselves and know how it is used. Thirty percent of annual giving takes place in December; 10 percent occurs during the last three days of the year.

An increasing number of individuals are responding to socially conscious social media efforts. More than half of all people who engage with nonprofits on social media end up donating money, volunteering, or attending or participating in a nonprofit-sponsored community event.

*Online Donations*

By online donations, I refer to receiving gifts via a dedicated webpage.

The main advantage of raising money through such contributions is that the barrier to entry is low. Any nonprofit can create a customized donation page. You can then use social media to drive traffic to your site and donation page.

Another advantage is that donor information is automatically recorded in your donor database. If it is properly executed, donating online makes for a simple and easy donor experience and ease of recordkeeping. Its speed and convenience reduce your fundraising costs. And the analytic tools available make it easy to monitor how the campaign is performing.

However, with so many online pleas for money, donor fatigue may set in—and with it a risk of losing donors. To stand out above the barrage of requests, online appeals must be targeted, imaginative, and immersive. For them to work, your agency needs a robust online audience, which may mean months or years of creating great content, developing your agency's reputation, and building your organization's online presence. You also run the risk of donors making small donations when there is potential for much more.

## Email Campaigns

Email campaigns have the advantage of low or no costs. They are easy to send to a large number of people. And they're quick. You can acquire new donors and volunteers through email campaigns faster than any other fundraising vehicle. Emails are easily customizable and personalized. It is also easy to track open, click-through, and response rates using email.

However, just as with online donations, there is a lot of noise to overcome. People may subscribe to your email list but not be engaged. Watch your engagement indicators and have someone on staff become an expert in capturing the recipients' attention.

## Direct Mail

Direct mail reaches donors who do not wish to make donations online or have limited access to computers and the internet, mainly older donors. Because some older donors would rather respond to email and it is cheaper to deliver than direct mail, know your donors. Not all older donors will prefer direct mail.

The primary advantage to direct mail fundraising is that you can put a lot of information in your letters, much more than in an email or text message. However, the printing and mailing costs add up. And the process of actually assembling personalized letters with self-addressed envelopes into their proper mailing envelope is laborious. And then there's the problem of your letter being perceived as junk mail. If you do a direct mail campaign, make sure that your envelope will stand out so that the recipients open it instead of throwing it away.

> **Food for Thought**
>
> To pursue donations from individuals, you can implement online giving structures, email campaigns, direct mail campaigns, phone-a-thons, text-to-give campaigns, crowdfunding efforts, peer-to-peer campaigns, major gift solicitations, planned gift structures, and donor-advised funds solicitations. Each comes with its own pros and cons.

*Phone-a-thons*

Soliciting by phone can be effective because of the personal contact involved. You can also follow up a direct mail campaign by phone and improve donor response rates. A phone-a-thon is also scalable. Through phone contact, you can increase your number of donors and gifts, welcome new donors, get lapsed donors back, improve donor retention, convert annual donors to monthly donors, thank donors, and get donor feedback. The personal contact can pay off.

However, it is labor-intensive. Soliciting by phone requires preparation, skill, a passion for the mission and agency, and good customer service skills. Many times you never reach the donor and must leave a message. Some donors are averse to phone solicitations, so if a caller is not tactful, they can do more harm than good. Because making the donation is not immediate, some people will not follow through with their pledges, unlike with online and email campaigns. You must budget for this.

*Text-to-Give Solicitations*

Like online and email campaigns, giving through a text-to-give option is easy and convenient. This option can be used to recruit new donors as well as reach existing ones. Most people use smartphones regularly so the channel can reach a broad audience. Little or no donor research is required. And you don't have to capture the recipients' attention for long. Donations given through text-to-give options are impulse choices, so the average gift is low.

However, software, licensing, and transaction fees can take up to 10 percent of total donations received. There is also a lag between when the donation is made and when the money is received. There is no built-in option for recurring gifts, and often there is a cap on the contribution. You also have no way of capturing donor data.

*Crowdfunding*

Crowdfunding is a way to promote your campaigns to a wide audience. GoFundMe is one example, of hundreds, of a crowdfunding site. You get small donations, but small donations add up. Set-up is free. Little time is required to connect with donors and realize gifts.

However, for this to work, you need a large audience. You must also be in constant communication with your donors, sharing progress updates and major and minor setbacks. It's time-consuming. Crowdfunding sites also charge fees. In addition, crowdfunding is a saturated market.

### Peer-to-Peer Campaigns

Peer-to-peer fundraising is a form of crowdfunding, where each fundraiser, usually a volunteer, sets up their own fundraising page and lends their personal voice to the cause, asking their connections to donate. Peer-to-peer campaigns are often an effective donor recruitment strategy, as your fundraisers reach donor pools inaccessible to you. It's cost-effective because it leverages your existing donor base, reducing your fundraising costs. Peer-to-peer campaigns also provide immediate social proof of the worthiness of your nonprofit.

However, it takes time and effort to train volunteer fundraisers on using the fundraising platform and how to make the ask. Someone will need to be available to troubleshoot with them and address their concerns. And it takes time to keep your fundraisers motivated. In addition, sometimes their communications are not quite on point, leading to inconsistent messaging. We talk about the importance of consistent messaging in **Chapter Nine**.

### Large Personal Gifts

Large gifts from individuals are most effectively garnered through individual solicitation, the most personal form of fundraising that exists. It's just harder to say no to a person face to face. What makes gifts "large" is defined by the nonprofit pursuing them. I've seen organizations where five hundred dollars is a large gift and others where large gifts don't start until you reach at least a million dollars.

Large gifts are often structured gifts, that is, given over a period of time. Usually, they are in the form of a bequest but not necessarily. A donor may defer a gift over time using other vehicles for tax purposes.

Usually, structured gifts require a long lead time for donor cultivation and to receive the gift itself. In addition to the donor, often families, attorneys, financial planners, and tax specialists are involved in the process. You may want to consider enlisting representatives from these industries as fundraising volunteers. You may also want to consider facilitating meetings that all the different advisors can attend at the same time. You want to be as helpful to the donor as possible.

However, garnering large gifts is labor- and time-intensive. And individual solicitations require a lot of planning and research on the fundraiser's part. In addition, your asker has to convey enthusiasm for what they are asking. Not just anyone can do it.

## Donor-Advised Funds

A donor-advised fund (DAF) is an irrevocable commitment to charity that a donor gives assets to for grantmaking purposes. The advantage of forming a DAF is that the donor is eligible for an immediate tax deduction.

To get DAF donations, you need to develop a relationship with the funds' donors, as opposed to a board of directors or program officer at a foundation. You can find donor contact information through a philanthropic advisor at your local community foundation. You also need to make it easy for the donors to recommend DAF grants to your nonprofit, meaning set it up so they can contribute in just a few clicks instead of going through their account manager. There are widgets available to put on your website that will make this possible.

Understand that donors cannot inure themselves in any way through a DAF, meaning they cannot purchase tickets to an event or receive any other benefits. The money in a DAF must be used solely for charitable purposes. And they can't make pledges, either, since they are not the legal owner of the fund. Instead, send them a letter of intent.

When you acknowledge their gift, do not use the standard tax-deductible language as the tax benefit was realized when the donor gave to the DAF, and the donor is not entitled to another deduction.

## Grants

Grants are gifts from institutions. Boards and staff like them because they are generally large gifts and can fund important client programs, advancing your nonprofit's mission.

However, getting them is time- and labor-intensive. Grant giving can be bureaucratic, particularly government grants. And the funds most often come with strings attached, as they are restricted in their use for the purposes outlined in the grant.

Grant funding is generally lumped into one category, be it foundation or government funding. There are huge differences, though, in the skill set needed to write and be awarded foundation grants and the skill set needed to write and win federal grants. That's why agencies responding to a government request for proposals often hire outside consultants to write their federal grant proposals.

### *Foundation Funding*

According to Foundation Source, the average foundation gift is twelve thousand dollars, a large gift as far as average donation amounts go. Which makes grant funding desirable to a lot of nonprofits. Like the 1.56 million nonprofits in the United States.

However, grant funding is highly competitive and time-intensive. Another drawback is that most foundation grants are given for only one year. Since they must be applied for every year, they are not a long-term reliable source of funding. Which means that it's hard to staff core programs on a long-term basis. It's hard to plan for growth because you never know who will fund your program for a second or subsequent year.

Foundations generally like to fund programs where most of the money is used for the direct benefit of the client. Rarely do they fund general operating expenses. Sometimes they won't even cover salaries. Which means if you get the grant to implement the program you wrote

> **Food for Thought**
>
> Be careful when applying for and accepting grant money, both foundation and government. Make sure you have a plan to cover total, not just direct, costs.

for, implementing that program may cost more than what you received. Yet, programs must continue to operate. Nonprofits shrink on the financial vine with a commitment to provide programming without their general and administrative expenses covered. I see it happen all the time. If you go for foundation funding, make sure that you have other revenue streams to supplement it.

*Government Contracts*

Government contracts are enticing because they offer large sums for important social programs your nonprofit may implement. However, government funding is associated with a bevy of risks.

The most direct threat to governmental funding is budget cuts. If government budgets are cut, you can end up with a reduction in the number or dollar amount of government contracts you have. Funding may be reduced, money may not become available for subsequent years, or there may be a complete elimination of funding. And new money may not be available to make up for the loss.

Also, during the application or renewal process, your contract is vulnerable to changes in budget allocations. Critical funding may be significantly delayed once you are approved for it. Then, too, if the allocations are eliminated, you may not get the funding at all, even if you were approved for it. You may face serious cash flow problems in those circumstances. Which causes other issues, such as your clients not receiving needed services. Or your program is no longer able to be fully staffed. In addition, if you stopped operations to deal with cash flow until funding is restored, you will still be required to meet your original contract performance objectives. Most governmental contracts do not start the date governmental budget negotiations are over. They start at the beginning of the federal, state, or local fiscal year.

Relying on government funding is a gamble. Don't put all your eggs in the government funding basket.

If you do pursue government grants, pay attention to how much the program will cost you to run. The allowable administrative expenses are often lower than the actual administrative expenses you incur. Which means you may have uncovered general and administrative expenses. Run the numbers to make sure your nonprofit can afford that.

Know *all* the requirements involved in applying for the grant, operating the program, reporting program results, and reporting financial results. Government regulations are stringent. Monitoring and reporting on governmental contracts can be onerous. Make sure you have the organizational capacity to handle such requirements.

Also, make sure you have enough money to meet any match requirements. If the contract is going to cost more than you will receive, don't apply. If you still apply, have a solid plan in place for covering unfunded expenses.

In addition, you will incur nonreimbursable preparation costs, mainly labor. Government grants are time-intensive to prepare with complex application requirements. It costs staff time to attend mandatory technical assistance sessions. You may also need to hire a fundraising consultant who specializes in applying for government grants. Beware, though, that these costs are not reimbursable.

Governmental funding may be a good idea. Or, after weighing the risks against the benefits, it may not.

## Corporate Giving

Philanthropy is good for business. According to Donor Box, corporate social responsibility research has consistently shown a positive relationship between sales and a company's social responsibility activities. According to Sustainable Brands, 81 percent of consumers will make personal sacrifices to buy from companies perceived as socially responsible.

Companies address the rising importance of philanthropy in building their brands, attracting talent, and engaging employees. Research shows a positive relationship between how employees perceive their company's contribution to the community and the employees' level of commitment to their work. According to Giving USA, 78 percent of employees want to be active in corporate social responsibility efforts.

Many donors who work give through workplace initiatives. More than 90 percent of companies offer an employee matching gift program.

To boost their contributions, many working donors take advantage of their employer's matching gift programs. Employees may also participate in workplace fundraisers or payroll deduction programs.

You can tap into corporate giving using a variety of approaches. Businesses give through employee matching gift programs, employee volunteer programs, in-kind or non-monetary donations, outright gifts, sponsorships, employee donor-advised funds, and corporate foundations. Often nonprofits can take advantage of several of the giving vehicles a business offers. For a more comprehensive look into corporate giving, see the **Nonprofit Quick Guide: Best-Kept Secrets to Engaging and Retaining Business Donors**.

### Food for Thought

There is so much more than event sponsorships and auction items you can ask for from businesses. Businesses give in various ways, including employee matching gift programs, employee volunteer programs, in-kind or non-monetary donations, outright gifts, sponsorships, employee donor-advised funds, and corporate foundations.

Fundraising events are a hybrid of individual and corporate giving. You raise money by selling tickets, selling personal ads for the ad journal, auctioning items, facilitating a raffle, and asking for donations while at the same time garnering sponsorships, asking for in-kind auction contributions, selling tickets, selling business ads for the ad journal. Usually, the affairs attract large numbers of people, raising your nonprofit's visibility and growing your mailing list. And they're fun, boosting camaraderie among donors and between staff and donors. Staff can meet new donors and deepen relationships with prospective donors. Donors get to put a name to a face, making the relationship more personal. Events can also boost your online fundraising efforts.

However, events are labor-intensive and often break even, at best, after labor costs are accounted for. They require detailed planning, some of which may unravel, putting stress on staff and guests. Attendance is subject to weather conditions. An unexpected weather event can cancel an event without much notice. Your event may also compete with other community events, decreasing interest or participation in your affair.

## Capital Campaigns

Capital campaigns utilize all forms of giving—individual, foundation, and corporate. Rather than being a separate form of giving, a capital campaign raises money over a specific period for large projects requiring a lot of capital, for example, purchasing or renovating a building, starting an endowment, or purchasing a large piece of equipment. Usually, capital campaigns take place over several years and involve hiring an outside consultant. When done well, capital campaigns raise substantial amounts of money, increase a nonprofit's visibility in the community, and increase the acquisition of annual gifts.

## In-kind Donations

In-kind donations are non-monetary donations. They are tangible things, like food, clothing, books, computers, furniture, or artwork. They have a monetary value, which you should research and track.

Sometimes, though, people or companies want to give you something your nonprofit can't use. And sometimes selling it is more hassle than it's worth. Which is one of the reasons your agency needs a gift acceptance policy. A gift acceptance policy will clearly state what can and cannot be accepted by the organization, giving you or your fundraiser a polite way to decline a donation. A sample gift acceptance policy is included in **Appendix A**.

## Let's Talk Technology

Instead of keeping your data in an Excel file, invest in a good donor management software system. There are hundreds on the market at all price levels.

When comparing costs, check how much they charge to convert your current data into the new system. And think about what you need the software to do, in addition to tracking donors and donations, such as grant, event, volunteer, or membership management. Different software packages integrate better with some software packages than others.

Think about your total needs. I have worked with nonprofits who chose software packages that integrate with an agency mailing list, event registration, grants calendar, and/or volunteer management system.

Ask for demonstrations from the software companies you are considering and talk to other users to find the right program for you.

When choosing fundraising software, make sure it:

- Is easy to understand how and where to enter data. As you grow, you may have multiple users entering data, and you want the entries to be uniform.

- Has a place to enter your fundraising goals. You want to be able to compare this year's goals to this year's performance and this year's performance to last year's performance.

- Allows you to analyze the performance of individual fundraising activities as well the four channels—individual, foundation, and corporate giving. You want to know what activities are performing best and who is responding to them.

- Contains enough space for multiple years of notes in a donor's profile.

- Has mail merge capabilities that can personalize the name, address, last donation amount, and this year's requested donation amount. Personalized appeals always perform better than impersonal ones.

- Can run donor and donation reports, including donor history, average gift per donor, donation growth, donor acquisition, and donor retention rates. You will want to be able to track what's going on year to date, compare year over year, and see trends.

- Tracks who entered what data, when. You want to be able to go back if you have questions or supervise someone who is doing the data input.

And build for the future. Expect fundraising growth. You want a donor software package that can grow with you.

A good constituent relationship management (CRM) system is nice to have and, many would argue, essential to have. A CRM system is a technology that manages your relationships and interactions with donors, potential donors, and other types of supporters. It helps nonprofits stay connected to their supporters, streamline fundraising and marketing processes, and improve net revenue.

A good CRM system for nonprofits will have features that increase donor relationship efficiencies. For example, automated email sequences, which save time when conducting large email campaigns. Or tracking of communication flows and response rates. Or metrics that calculate the conversion rates from one step in the flow to the next.

Software today can cater to marketing endeavors with an added adaptation for fundraising analysis or fundraising endeavors with an added adaptation for marketing analysis. In other words, you can find donor management systems on some CRM software and CRM systems on some donor management software.

Both donor management and CRM software can come with all kinds of bells and whistles. You probably don't need them all. What you want depends on what type of fundraising you're doing and what you need to be integrated with what.

## Bringing It Together

Hone your and your development staff's communication, planning, time management, and negotiating skills. They are essential for garnering donations from individual, foundation, corporate, and government donors. Each fundraising method has a set of pros and cons. Account for them when considering different activities. Remember, each fundraising technique also has its own pros and cons Once you implement your activities, invest in the most robust technology you need to effectively track donations and monitor trends. You want your fundraising infrastructure to grow as your fundraising program grows.

## Points to Remember

- There are many ways to raise money. They include online donations, direct mail, phone-a-thons, text-to-give solicitations, crowdfunding, peer-to-peer campaigns, major and planned gifts, donor-advised funds, foundation grants, government contracts, employee matching gifts, sponsorships, special events, capital campaigns, in-kind donations, and volunteer hours. Which method you choose depends on your skills, organizational capacity, and strategic goals.

- Invest in donor management software that is easy to understand how and where to enter data. Make sure it has a place to enter your fundraising goals; allows you to analyze the performance of single campaigns and by fundraising channel; contains enough space for multiple years of notes; has mail merge capabilities that can personalize the name, address, last donation amount, and this year's requested donation amount; can run donor and donation reports including donor history, average gift per donor, donation growth, donor acquisition, and donor retention rates; and tracks who entered what data when.

## What's Next?

In the next chapter, we move to step two of The Sustainable High ROI Fundraising System, empowering your board. To fully understand the three remaining steps of the system, I recommend reading the following chapters in the order presented. However, when you are ready to implement the system, steps two, three, and four are executed concurrently.

## Chapter Six

# Empowering Your Board

Your board is the most valuable leadership asset your nonprofit has. Board members teach the community how to interact with your agency. The board is where an infectious fundraising culture starts. During step two of The Sustainable High ROI Fundraising System, you help your board become comfortable with fundraising. You build their skills so they become strong and consistent mission ambassadors to the community. You then build on their efforts to leverage existing resources.

Results you can expect after implementing this step are:

- Board leadership that promotes your nonprofit to the community
- A leadership culture that enables you and your staff to capitalize on your nonprofit's fundraising assets and the strong community support board members have created
- Board and staff leaders who work together in a supportive relationship for fundraising

## Why Board Members Don't Fundraise

Is your board excited about fundraising? Probably not. They may think that fundraising and governance don't have anything to do with one another. They may see fundraising as management's responsibility, with their role only holding staff accountable for financial results. Or they may get bogged down in the details of event planning or wordsmithing the annual appeal.

Board members are often reluctant to fundraise because:

- They are afraid of rejection.

- They think they will have to reciprocate in the same way they are asking the donor to give.

- They don't understand that 90 percent of fundraising is not about the ask.

- They don't have a good role model to learn from.

The good news is that you can change things by getting your board excited about fundraising. The trick is in onboarding new members properly. Focus on fundraising strategy instead of monetary transactions. Give them the tools that make fundraising a transformational experience for both them and those they are approaching. Give them fundraising tasks that result in appreciation of their efforts.

### Warning!

If your board members' fundraising is centered around reciprocal asks, often manifested in board members being asked to sell tickets to an event, you have a disaster in the making. Not only will your nonprofit not raise as much money as it could, but the board will be caught up in fundraising details that distract them from the true work of governance.

## Recruit Them Correctly

An ounce of prevention is worth a pound of cure. The number one thing you can do to avoid poor engagement in fundraising is to fully explain the role of board members before they say yes. Discuss a board member's fiduciary responsibilities as trustees of the organization—that board members are legal stewards of the public trust. And then talk about what that means in practical terms. Set crystal clear expectations.

For example, as part of their fiduciary duties, board members must provide financial oversight of the nonprofit. Understanding fundraising strategy and monitoring its implementation is an essential part of overseeing financial success. Board members must also ensure there are adequate resources to carry out the agency's purpose, in other words, to fulfill its mission. Fundraising is all about garnering resources. In addition, board members are entrusted with the responsibility to strengthen programs and services, expanding mission in the community. It is fundraising growth that fuels such expansion.

Let your board members know what they are getting upfront. Link their legal and fiduciary roles as trustees directly to the fundraising responsibilities you expect them to fulfill. And tell them why what you are asking them to do is important. It's lives you're changing.

## Focus on Strategy

Board members may not think of fundraising as part of strategic governance. Or they see fundraising as solely management's responsibility. Or they get caught up in all the fundraising details, not knowing the difference between governance and management. In these cases, teach them what governance is: setting policy for and determining the organization's strategic direction and assuring its design, creation, and accountability.

For example, a board approves a strategic plan, of which fundraising is part. The staff, through the executive director, implement the plan and report on their progress in meeting their goals. The board approves a gift acceptance policy. Staff develop and implement procedures in line with that policy. (A sample gift acceptance policy can be found in **Appendix A**.) The board approves the annual budget, which includes fundraising revenue goals and cost allocations. Staff are responsible for implementing those fundraising activities and keeping costs down. As civic leaders, the board primes the community for staff to be successful. As organizational leaders, the board also teaches the community how to interact with the nonprofit they serve regarding programs, services, advocacy, and fundraising.

Then talk strategy, not implementation. Talk about fundraising as a strategy to meet goals you have set together instead of money transactions that need to happen. Let your board set your fundraising strategy and let the staff build and implement the work plans. Strategy falls under governance duties. Work plans fall under staff duties.

## Engage Them in Creating Transformations

To really excite your board about fundraising, focus on a transformational fundraising strategy rather than a transactional one. If your board is reluctant to fundraise, you may be giving board members transactional fundraising tasks to oversee, like asking for money and monitoring revenues. Instead, show them the transformational power of fundraising. Don't worry about them overseeing specific fundraising activities. Show them how they are contributing to the progress of changing lives.

### Shifting Mindset

To excite your board about fundraising, set expectations up front. Focus on revenue strategy rather than operations. Engage them to create transformations rather than making transactions possible. Give them tasks where they will hear appreciation for their efforts. And teach them how to fulfill their roles as leaders to the community.

Think progress versus work. Work is comprised of the tasks you complete to get a job done. There may or may not be anything exciting about them. Just completing tasks is not very motivational. And completing tasks in and of themselves does not lead to feeling a part of a larger purpose.

Seeing progress toward meeting goals, on the other hand, is motivating. It shows people how what they do fits into the big picture. It gives them a sense of purpose.

If you're asking your board to give because they signed on the dotted line, oversee fundraising activities that make money, or ask their network to give because your nonprofit needs money, you are asking them to perform work.

On the other hand, if you show them how their giving will enhance community giving, oversee the organization's financial and mission growth, and give their network an opportunity to provide life-changing experiences, you ask them to contribute to progress.

The trick is reporting back to them the success of their efforts. Let them see how they are contributing to progress. Give them purpose. Excite them about what they can and have accomplished.

The same is true when it comes to your donors. Asking them to write a check to meet financial obligations is mundane work. Asking them to change a life is transformational. You must, however, report back on the results of what you asked them to do. That way, they can see progress, how their actions fit into the big picture, and gain a sense of purpose.

## Give Them Tasks that Result in Appreciation of Their efforts.

We all want to be acknowledged and appreciated. Create opportunities for board members to just say thank you to donors. And create opportunities for your donors to show appreciation of board members' leadership. An excellent way to accomplish this is through a board-driven donor thank-a-thon. Your donors and your board have at least one thing in common—passion for your nonprofit. Find ways that work for donors and board members to share their joint passion and mutual appreciation of one another.

## Help Them Lead by Example

It is board members who teach the community how to interact with the nonprofit they represent. They set the example.

Before giving, many foundations and major donors ask about board giving. These potential donors want to know that the leaders are so dedicated to the mission that they put their money where their mouth is. It is not enough for board members to only serve. They are also expected to financially support the agency. Major funders expect board members to lead by example.

Because of the importance of board giving to fundraising success, every nonprofit should have a board giving policy. Some policies state a minimum expected donation. Others say any gift is acceptable as long as there is 100 percent board giving. My favorite is to ask board members to make the nonprofit they are governing one of the top three charities they give to. That way, you don't exclude poorer community members from serving, and all board members have an opportunity to participate at a sacrificial level, no matter what their income level. You can find a sample board giving policy in **Appendix A**.

## Evaluate Strategies, Not Operations

The board's role in fundraising is strategic rather than operational. Your board members should not be planning events or wordsmithing appeals. Their job is not to manage the processes and oversee implementation. That's your job as executive director. The board's job is to strategically allocate resources and monitor their acquisition. They should be asking questions like:

- Are we fulfilling our duties to provide resources to implement and grow our mission?

- What strategies are we going to allocate resources toward to meet our mission?

- Do we have a written updated strategic plan that we regularly review and update?

- Are we constantly promoting mission in all we do, even in our fundraising strategy?

- Have we provided a favorable environment for the executive director and staff to succeed in raising money? For example, do we have written board giving and gift acceptance policies in place that we enforce?

- Where will we realize the most financial and mission return on our investment in fundraising?

- How do we want the community to interact with us? How do we as a board influence them to respond the way we want them to?

- Are we making progress in meeting our mission and financial goals?

Notice that these are strategic, not operational, questions. The board's job is to focus on governance and strategy and provide an environment that supports the executive director and staff in executing the strategies they have deemed most effective. It is the executive director's and staff's jobs to abide by the policies the board has set and implement the activities that fulfill the strategic objectives the board has set. It is the role of the executive to translate operational measurements from the staff into strategic ones from the board so that the board can evaluate the organization's performance in meeting its mission.

## Surmount Board Misconceptions

Ever heard anything like the following? I have.

- "If we could only get more grants."
- "Agency X raised $100,000 through its event. Why can't we do the same thing?"
- "Let's raise the money by holding another event!"
- "Why can't the development director do it? After all, that's what she was hired to do."
- "Fundraising is not a board's job. We leave that to the professionals."

If your board members say things like the above statements to you, they are not thinking strategically about fundraising. They are thinking transactionally. Their concern is on the transactions it takes to raise money.

Don't fault your board members. They are trying to be helpful. Most of them think in terms of big government grants and special events because that's all the fundraising they've been exposed to. They may not know anything else. They are doing their best to offer ideas for how the organization can raise resources to raise the money the agency so desperately needs.

Obviously, statements like those above are not helpful. As we have seen, you need diversified revenue streams to spread risk. And many factors affect revenue mix decisions and the success of any one fundraising element. We saw in **Chapter Five** the different costs to raise one dollar and the different returns on investment you can realize. As overseers of mission fulfillment and growth, the board are very much concerned with fundraising, whether they realize it or not.

Don't answer them with the details behind operations. And don't let your development person either. You will sound like you are defending yourself and may be perceived as argumentative or impeding progress. They certainly will not feel heard or that their input is appreciated.

Instead, answer with strategic questions about fundraising, like the ones we mentioned previously. Give them the knowledge they need to make informed strategic decisions.

## Overcome Fundraising Resistance

Fundraising is a charged word, and there are different perceptions of what it means. Many of them are negative and tinged with the fear of asking for money. Board members are no different. In my experience, most board members cringe when you ask them to raise money. Some refuse outright.

My suggestion is to not call it fundraising. Instead, break the fundraising tasks you want to accomplish down to their lowest denominator and ask people to complete those tasks instead. For example, don't ask your board members to recruit new donors. Ask them to talk about your agency's mission with their friends and colleagues as the situation arises. Then you can periodically check with them about who was excited about the mission and would be a good person to reach out to. Don't ask your board members to ask for money. Ask them to talk about the agency's progress in meeting and growing its mission. Again, refer interested people to you. You can work with your fundraising staff to reach out and make the ask. You don't have to ask your board members to do something they don't want to do. Ask them to do something they love to do—being involved in meeting the agency's mission.

That's not to say board members don't support staff efforts to reach the goals the board has set. They do. For example, personalizing appeal letters with a handwritten note or participating in a donor thank-a-thon are excellent ways board members can support staff efforts.

### Clarifying Point

All your board members need to do to help fundraise is to be enthusiastic mission ambassadors for your organization.

Thanking donors is a great task to ask board members to do. The donors feel appreciated being contacted by top leadership, while board members get a real sense of why donors donate and what excites them about being involved with the agency. Usually, board members are rejuvenated by such feedback. Just make sure that you, as executive director, capture that information and share it with your development staff.

Sometimes board members don't participate because they are given too much to do. They may not feel comfortable saying "no," or they say "yes" and then report back that they were unable to complete the assignment. Don't overload and de-motivate. Set realistic goals and expectations. Don't set your board members up for failure. If you do, you will never get them to fundraise for you.

## Getting the Most out of Empowering Your Board

It is thrilling to see your board really doing what they signed up to do: support your agency in promoting its mission. And you are making it a rewarding experience for them. How great is that? The board is eagerly promoting your nonprofit's mission in the community. And leading other supporters to do the same. It's an infectious cycle. With a development plan based on your nonprofit's unique combination of fundraising assets and board members strategically engaged in fundraising, you end up with an organizational culture that enables you and your staff to financially capitalize on the buzz your board is creating.

You can't just empower the board and leave it at that, though. You need to mobilize your staff too. That way, the board and staff work together in a supportive relationship for fundraising, and everyone is on the same page, receiving the same messages to repeat to the community. We talk about mobilizing your staff in **Chapter Seven**. We cover messaging in **Chapter Nine**.

## How It Worked in Real Life

Of course, easier said than done. Here are some examples of how it worked with the four organizations we highlighted in **Chapter Three**.

## Regional First Responder Assistance Agency

The end goal here was to increase donations and appeal to a younger cohort. The task regarding the board was to get them more involved in fundraising. One hundred percent of them gave. So, it was just a matter of helping them feel comfortable reaching out and recruiting younger donors. To do that, we needed to build on the organization's strong volunteer structure, and that started with the board.

We started with candid talks about fundraising. We didn't ask board members to fundraise. We asked them to share their experiences of how and why they got involved with the agency, why they stayed, and why they got more involved. We needed to get off this quid pro quo mentality of "if you donate to my cause, I'll donate to yours." We practiced sharing stories then asked them to share the story with five people and report on results. Most board members reported positive experiences, which encouraged other board members to also reach out.

It worked because we asked them to share their enthusiasm for the mission and not their need for money. The money was just the vehicle to better serve the mission.

## Statewide Domestic Violence Transitional Housing Agency

Since the executive director interacted directly with the board in this agency, the development director and I needed to develop nontraditional avenues to get the board involved in fundraising. Which meant disseminating information to the executive director about funding requirements for board giving. Because so many foundations required it, the board, interested in raising as many additional resources as possible, bought into 100 percent board giving.

The development director and I then formed a fundraising committee managed by the development director. We invited board members, donors, and clients to join the committee. Intrigued, a few board members did. Because they were interacting with clients, the committee members saw how additional resources changed people's lives in a very real way. Because they were involved with donors, board members got a real sense of why people gave. And they got excited about it. And started sharing their enthusiasm with other board members. Which excited them to share with their friends. Soon board members were bringing the names of their community connections to the executive director, who shared them with the development department.

## Community Drug Prevention Agency

The board members here were concerned about the declining revenues, as well they should have been. They saw the agency's survival at stake. Closing the doors was not an option since they felt their mission was so important in the community. The board was acutely aware of how their services changed people's lives.

After straightening out the recordkeeping, the first thing the executive director did was present a true picture of the agency's circumstances to the board. We then worked with the board to set fundraising policies and institute stronger accountability controls. The next thing we did was to allocate resources for a new fundraising software system. The agency now had the infrastructure in place to accommodate stronger fundraising endeavors.

We spent quite a bit of time listening to board member objections to participating in fundraising. So, we didn't ask them to fundraise. Instead, we focused on keeping the mission going, which necessarily involved raising money. We took asking for dollars out of the board equation, moving it to the new executive director, who had a solid background in fundraising.

We also worked on developing their fundraising leadership. We shared funding requirements regarding board giving, and the executive director brought donor inquiries about board giving to board meetings. Soon, the board adopted a 100 percent board giving policy. They directed the executive director to revise their board recruitment materials and put in board donation reporting protocols. They also changed their board service requirements, making not contributing a reason for termination of board membership.

As the board modeled giving leadership, skeptical donors were encouraged to continue contributing to the organization. Soon, others' fears were also allayed. Which encouraged more donors to contribute.

### International Maternal Health Education Agency

In this situation, the board had its hands full in the middle of an executive search. The search took priority. So, we decided to prepare the board for fundraising for the incoming executive director.

The first task was convincing the board of the need to invest in fundraising when things were currently going well—the agency was growing, and demand for services was high. So, we developed a board training that showed the need for unrestricted monies, defined fundraising in terms of mission fulfillment, explained foundation and major donor inquiries, and made the case for investment in fundraising. As is to be expected, there was quite a discussion around board giving.

The board responded well to the training, asking that the conversation about fundraising be continued at future meetings.

## Bringing It Together

A nonprofit board has a fiscal duty to make sure that resources are raised and allocated to meet the organization's mission. Many times, board members don't realize their responsibility to be involved in fundraising. Board members may also have unrealistic ideas about fundraising and are reluctant to fundraise. And they may confuse board and staff fundraising roles.

You can change things. Teach them what they need to know about fundraising and their responsibilities for it. With proper recruitment, focus on strategy, and engagement in progress, you will see your board get and stay excited about fundraising. You will have board members who understand their roles in fundraising, embrace it, and actively do their part to garner resources to meet the mission they care about.

## Points to Remember

- Boards have a legal responsibility to make sure resources are available for mission achievement. Prepare your board to fundraise by properly recruiting members, focusing them on strategy, and engaging them in creating life-changing transformations.

- Help your board members lead by example. Share board giving inquiries that come from other donors with your board.

- Develop a board giving policy that allows for participation and sacrificial giving no matter what the income level. One way to do that is to have a mandatory board giving policy that sets a top-three-charities donation level.

- To overcome objections to fundraising, don't call it fundraising. Start by breaking down the steps of an ask into specific details. Don't focus on the money you are trying to raise. Instead, focus on the progress in mission fulfillment the organization has achieved through added financial support.

## What's Next

The board sets fundraising policy and analyzes financial performance. You, the executive director, and the development staff implement the board's policies and are responsible for achieving the financial goals the board has set. In the next chapter, we talk about how to set your development staff up for success in meeting the monetary goals they have been given.

## Chapter Seven

# Mobilizing Your Staff

To mobilize your staff to achieve fundraising success, you create an environment conducive to fundraising and give your staff the tools necessary to meet the financial and mission goals you and the board have identified as priorities. This chapter talks about how you can leverage the never-enough resources available to you to reach those goals. You want to spread mission while realizing the highest net income and return on investment possible.

To implement the system efficiently, you work with the staff and board concurrently. Together, they spread your nonprofit's message, advancing its mission.

Results you can expect after implementing this step:

- More donors
- Higher donations
- Reduced fundraising costs
- A development work plan that encompasses total fundraising operations, including technology, communications, campaigns and appeals, staffing, and board involvement

## Establish a Mission Mindset

Always put the mission first. Always. And train your staff to put the mission first. No matter what the fundraising activity. It is the mission that motivates people to enter into donor relationships with your organization. Individuals want to make a positive impact on an issue they care about.

Foundations exist to fund nonprofits that can fulfill their mission. Businesses like to associate themselves with nonprofits with strong corporate identities, that is, nonprofits that ooze mission. If you want to connect with a potential donor, ensure your agency is all about its mission in everything it says and does. Put mission first and the money will follow.

## Set SMART Goals

When planning, make your staff's goals SMART (specific, measurable, action-oriented, realistic, and time-bound). This holds true whether the goals for your staff relate to authoring your strategic plan, creating an annual development plan, crafting a fundraising appeal, or stating program objectives in a grant proposal. What gets measured gets done. The SMARTer your goals, the more successful your team will be in meeting them.

Raising as much money as possible is not a SMART goal. Set volume and participation goals for each type of fundraising you do, including annual appeals, large personal gifts, grant proposals, corporate sponsorships, and special events.

To set realistic goals, ask, "What have we been able to achieve?" If your team raised only $250,000 in fundraising revenues over the past year and you or they budget to raise $1 million this upcoming year, chances are they will fail. Look at a year's worth of monthly trends. Analyze your revenue trends and associate each rise or dip with actions your agency took in response to the declining fundraising income. Look at what worked and what didn't work. Have your staff do more of what worked and not do what didn't work, no matter how beloved that activity is.

You also need to account for external economic trends. What is the environment you operate in? You may want to grow your fundraising exponentially, but what really is realistic given the current state of affairs?

In addition to overall dollars raised, calculate the average gift per donor. When you look at your number of donors, look at the number of new donors, repeat donors, and donors lost through attrition. The next time you execute a particular fundraising activity, try increasing the average gift per donor and donor retention rate in addition to increasing the number of new donors.

Evaluate your monthly and annual staff fundraising performance using the metrics you stated in your goals. Once they meet their existing goals, set new, higher goals. And be SMART about them.

## Focus on Net Income

Total dollars raised, or gross income, is probably the most common way people measure fundraising success. Gross income is total revenues raised. Board members and executive directors are often dazzled by these numbers. The number can be impressive if gross income is used as the basis for measuring fundraising success. But gross income does not paint the most accurate picture.

To really know if the activity raised money or not, you must talk about net income. It doesn't matter how much gross income your staff raised because it's net income that's important. Net income is revenues minus costs. You can eat up all your gross income in costs if you're not careful.

For example, I once interacted with a nonprofit that raised $1 million a year through its gala. Its leaders didn't understand why, with such great results, they were losing money in their overall budget every year. An analysis of their costs revealed that although they were raising $1 million each year, it took $1.25 million to raise it, meaning they lost a quarter-million dollars each year. I can give example after example of this occurring.

Don't let this happen at *your* nonprofit. Have your staff run the numbers. Be aware of your costs. Sometimes the activity raises more money just by reducing costs. If you want to *really* know how much your staff are raising, calculate net income. Take into account the costs and have the staff create a budget to realize positive net income.

## Avoid These Mistakes

Budget for success. Create an organizational budget that makes it easy for your staff to meet their goals. Don't set them, or your nonprofit, up for failure. Avoid these common mistakes when you budget.

## Overestimating Potential Revenues

One of the most common mistakes I see when creating budgets is overestimating potential revenues. Both development directors and executive directors do it. Projected fundraising revenues should not be based on any revenue deficit either of you is trying to fill. Don't base them on what the development team raised last year increased by an arbitrary percentage, either. Nor should you or your development director base projections on another organization's fundraising results. Both overall and fundraising revenue budgets need to be customized to *your* nonprofit's particular situation.

With the participation of your development director, develop fundraising goals that account for your nonprofit's and development team's capacity, economic environment, and unique growth history. For example, are your staff or volunteers burned out? Have there been layoffs? Have costs been cut? Is the economy in your community better or worse? Are residents moving in or out of your area? Any or all of these situations impact how much money your team can raise through any one activity.

It is good practice to budget revenues lower than projected in case something happens and your development team cannot perform as well as expected. When you do come up with reasonably projected revenues, decrease them by 5 percent. Leave room for results to be lower than anticipated.

## Underestimating Future Costs

Underestimate revenues but overestimate costs. Expenses are easier to project than revenues because they are more constant. However, you want to project them higher than you expect so that you have money available if your bills come in higher than expected.

> **Warning!**
>
> Common mistakes I see executive directors and boards make are overestimating projected fundraising revenues, not accounting for total and future costs, failing to compare the returns on investment of the available options, relying too much on one or two revenue streams, budgeting to only break even, and focusing heavily on donor acquisition instead of donor retention.

Plus, it leaves a little extra room if revenues are lower than expected. To counteract the uncertainty, take what you think will be an expected increase in costs and add 5 percent.

## Only Including Direct Expenses

And it's not only direct expenses that count. It is total costs you and your development director need to be concerned with. A good example of where development directors don't account for total costs is in their individual fundraising endeavors, especially grants and special events. I often see grant budgets with no acknowledgment of the indirect costs incurred, so the nonprofit ends up spending more money on the program than it takes in. The agency ends up constantly losing money. The same with special events. The average cost to raise a dollar through special events is 50 cents, *not including labor.* And special events are usually labor-intensive. These labor costs are rarely included in budgets or their analyses. Have your development director run the numbers accounting for labor and see how much you really make. If your agency is like most nonprofits, you actually lose money on your special events. Budget for total costs so that you are not making up for a constant loss.

## Failure to Compare Returns on Investment

Return on investment is calculated by dividing revenues by expenses. It tells you how hard your dollars are working for you, that is, how many dollars your agency can realize per each dollar you invest in that activity.

Some activities yield better results than others. For example, the average return on investment for major gifts is 900 percent, while the average return on investment for special events, not including labor expenses, is 50 percent. Too many nonprofits depend on special events, not their greatest return on investment, especially when factoring in labor costs. Compare the returns on your investment for each fundraising element you would like your development director to implement. See which ones yield the highest financial returns and consider investing your dollars there.

## Failure to Diversify Revenue Streams

When times are good, it is easy to rely on a steady stream of funding. Overreliance on one funding source is not healthy. Your nonprofit is in the danger zone when 80 percent or more of your fundraising revenue comes from one source. And I mean that in terms of broad revenue channels as well as individual activities within each channel.

There are four broad ways to realize revenue: earned income, or fees for service or product; unearned income, usually interest and dividends on investments; fundraising, that is, donations, grants, and special events; and government contracts. Studies show that nonprofits with two or more general revenue channels are more stable than those with one. On a macro level, you will do best with a more diversified funding mix.

You also need to look at the individual elements within each channel. For example, if you rely on government contracts, are they from more than one federal agency? Do they include state or local government sources? Or, if you rely on fundraising, are all your eggs in the grants basket? If so, you need to diversify your sources of funding so that if one revenue source dips, for whatever reason, it won't devastate your organization.

We talk about the roles and responsibilities of various fundraising staff members in **Chapter Seven**.

## Break-Even Budgeting

Sometimes, nonprofits think they cannot budget for a surplus, that they should only raise as much money as they need for the budget year. That's a mistake; you and your development director need to budget for surpluses. It's how your nonprofit grows.

The only exception to this rule is that grant revenue and expense budgets should show break-even income, including the donation you're asking for, because you want to show that you need exactly the amount of money you're requesting. Other than that, budget to make a surplus.

A healthy agency surplus is 3 to 6 percent of your operating budget. Your departmental, program, and event or activity budgets may individually be different, though. That's okay—they're all for different purposes. Make sure they maintain internal integrity with your overall budget.

### Failure to Set Aside a Portion of Surplus Income

When you do realize a surplus, don't just spend it. Build wealth as well as net income. Put one-third of your surplus away toward reserves for unexpected emergencies. Put one-third toward investing in your staff and improving infrastructure that streamlines processes and procedures, saving time and money in the long term. And invest one-third in long-term appreciating assets, so you have capital in case you ever need to borrow. It doesn't matter the amount. Just save regularly. Build wealth *and* net income so that you have the needed resources for your staff to function optimally.

## Focus on Donor Retention

The average first-time donor retention rate hovers around 25 percent. That means, on average, for every one hundred new donors acquired this year, seventy-five will not give again next year. And, on average, it costs about six times more to acquire a new donor than retain one. Which means most nonprofits are spending a lot of resources recruiting new donors that never give again. An emphasis on donor retention may serve you better. While you do need an emphasis on donor recruitment, generally you need more emphasis on donor retention.

To show how improved donor retention affects fundraising results, consider the following example where raising fifty thousand dollars results in more organizational income than raising a hundred thousand dollars.

| | Amount Raised | Average cost to Raise $1 | Total Cost to Raise | **Final Results** |
|---|---|---|---|---|
| 50% retained donors | $50,000 | $0.20 | $10,000 | $40,000 |
| 50% new donors | $50,000 | $1.20 | $60,000 | ($10,000) |
| Total | **$100,000** | - | $70,000 | *$30,000* |

| | Amount Raised | Average cost to Raise $1 | Total Cost to Raise | **Final Results** |
|---|---|---|---|---|
| 80% retained donors | $40,000 | $0.20 | $8,000 | $32,000 |
| 20% new donors | $10,0000 | $1.20 | $11,200 | ($1,200) |
| Total | **$50,000** | - | $19,200 | *$30,800* |

When your development director lays out their fundraising plans, make sure one of their goals addresses donor retention. And when you have them develop a fundraising budget, make sure they include resources allocated to improving your donor retention rate. If your agency spends more money recruiting than retaining a donor (which is the case for most nonprofits), which is more cost-effective—recruiting or retaining donors? The most cost-beneficial fundraising technique your development team can implement for your organization to realize increased revenues is usually improving the donor retention rate.

Don't get me wrong. You need to recruit new donors every year as there will always be some donor attrition, just because donors' lives change. You must acquire new donors. But don't do it at the expense of your current donors. Retaining donors is just as important as acquiring new ones.

## Collaborate with Others

Resources are scarce. There is more need than resources to meet the need. Your nonprofit can leverage its scarce resources, including staff efforts, by developing partnerships with others. In addition to greater mission fulfillment, partnerships can lead to reduced costs and help your nonprofit raise its visibility in the community, attracting people to your cause. People who can then be cultivated to become donors by your development team.

Both for-profits and nonprofits can make good partners. Organizations with similar missions can make great advocacy partners. You often find these kinds of partnerships through industry-based membership groups, such as the Child Welfare League of America or Chamber of Commerce. Partnerships with organizations whose missions complement yours can help provide wrap-around services to clients, such as an agreement between a grocery store and community food bank or a hospital and counseling center. Shared-space arrangements and office supply cooperatives are good examples of how agencies with similar needs can work together. Often-overlooked partnerships are those between organizations with similar markets. Corporate sponsorships are good examples of organizations with similar markets working together.

Partnerships help your development staff achieve their goals. Collaboration through partnerships, when done correctly, greatly benefit your development team, nonprofit, the partnering organization, and the community.

## Paint the Big Picture

It's so easy to get caught up in all the details, to get so involved in the day-to-day tasks that you lose sight of the big picture. And the big picture is, "Are we fulfilling and growing our mission?"

### Evaluate Total Success

When you evaluate your fundraising results, the three most important questions to ask are:

1. Did we promote the mission?

2. Did we make money? and

3. Did we strengthen important relationships?

### Food for Thought

When you evaluate
fundraising success, ask:

1. Did we promote the mission?

2. Did we make money?

3. Did we strengthen important
relationships?"

Since fundraising is all about mission, an essential component of evaluating your development team's performance is the results of the activity in furthering your organization's mission.

The mission should be the central focus in creating a fundraising plan and schedule of activities. You shouldn't make assessments based solely on net income. Are your fundraising endeavors designed to promote mission as well as make money? How successful was the implementation of the mission? Remember, mission first. The money follows the mission. Let your staff know that the mission, not money, comes first. Believe me, the money follows.

But fundraising is about raising money, too. Money is essential. It's the money that pays for the implementation of the mission.

When you look at the dollars raised, look at how your fundraising program did overall within a year and how much each fundraising channel and activity brought in. Thoroughly analyze your staff's results on both the micro and macro levels. That way, you can see overall how your team performed while comparing the financial performance of each channel and activity and start to get a feel for what is working for you and what is not.

The core of successful fundraising is relationship building. Fundraisers raise money by creating relationships between donors, your nonprofit, and your cause and talking to them about mission fulfillment and growth. The stronger the relationships you can build between donors and your agency, the more lucrative the relationship will be in dollars and cents. When evaluating the success of fundraising endeavors, always ask how the activities built stronger relationships with your donors, volunteers, advocates, collaborators, and community. The stronger the relationships your staff can build, the more vested people are in your agency, the more money comes into your agency.

## Give Them a Complete View

Fundraising touches almost all parts of a nonprofit: program, finance, IT, marketing, communications, volunteer training and management, and board relations. As such, fundraising staff members work most efficiently when they are aware of changes within your agency. They also perform most effectively when they are aware of the total needs of the organization so that they can direct energies toward securing the resources that best meet those needs.

Also, share what is going on within your agency partnerships, including your vendor relationships. A good fundraiser will go after any business or professional contacts that are candidates to be potential donors. Which is, at first, everyone your nonprofit has a relationship with. You want to make sure you present a consistent front to these contacts throughout the organization. For example, you don't want a potential wealthy business donor to be asked for a low donation. Nor do you want your development staff to approach a vendor with whom you have terminated a relationship. I've seen both happen.

## Getting the Most out of Mobilizing Your Staff

Set your fundraising staff up for success. Give them clear direction by setting SMART goals. Create both donation and donor goals. Fundraisers like to be liked. They will strive to meet their goals, especially if you properly motivate them. If you use SMART goals, it will also be easier for you to evaluate fundraising performance.

Be realistic when communicating and budgeting your revenue objectives. Develop revenue projections based on well-thought-through expenses, not a deficit based on a dream or arbitrary percentage increases. Don't motivate your fundraising staff to leave by creating impossible goals. You don't want the revolving door we talk about in **Chapter Eight**.

So that your nonprofit realizes a surplus, focus on net, not gross, income. Talk net income as well when you interview candidates or report back to the board about your agency's fundraising success.

Include total, not just direct costs, in your calculations so that you can compare the returns on investment for the different fundraising activities. By focusing on those fundraising elements with the highest financial return, you will expend the least amount of resources to achieve your goals, reducing your overall fundraising costs.

Remember your revenue mix, though. It's not all about return on investment. The purpose of fundraising activities includes more than financial goals. Mission promotion and relationship building are also important considerations.

Come from a mission mindset. Put the mission first. It is the mission that inspires people to give. It is the fulfillment of the mission that motivates people to give again. If you want more donors and higher gifts, talk about the mission and mission fulfillment. We cover how to attract donors to your cause in **Chapter Nine**.

And let your development staff operate in the big picture. Fundraising touches many organizational units, including program, finance, planning, marketing, communications, IT, and board relations. They will need to interact with many people to build a sustainable fundraising action plan that addresses total fundraising operations.

## How It Worked in Real Life

What did this look like in real life? How did the four nonprofits we've been following use these strategies to provide the tools their staff needed to successfully raise money?

### Regional First Responder Assistance Agency

This agency was trying to increase revenues, mainly through the acquisition of younger and business donors. But since it costs more to recruit a donor than retain one, we first looked at their donor retention rate and what we could do to move their existing donors up the donor ladder. To ask for higher donations, we changed their annual appeal letters, including adding more personalization. We also looked at their major giving program. They had already defined their major gift levels and created supporting materials. Now it was just a matter of asking people to give at higher levels.

Board members were already giving at major gift levels, so they had the giving leadership they needed. The staff's job was to support the volunteers doing the organization's work: fundraising, grant allocation, and volunteer recruitment. The agency already had a robust structure that exposed its volunteers to its mission in action. So, there was good volunteer motivation. It needed more hands on deck to acquire the number of younger and business donors it desired, paving the way to ask for new donations. We decided to tap into the large volunteer base to get more people asking their connections to participate in the mission, not asking for money.

To do this, staff needed to revise their volunteer recruitment, training, and leadership development materials to include messages volunteers could use when talking about the nonprofit or their volunteer work at the organization. The messages needed to be consistent with those the board members were hearing. That way, everyone was on the same page, and the board, staff, and volunteers would communicate consistent messages.

Another suggestion was investing in new fundraising software. The current software could not accommodate a large influx of new donors well. Several excellent, low-cost options on the market would fit their needs.

Since the staff could not do everything at once, we ranked the priorities based on the annual calendar of activities, cost outlay of the intervention, and cash flow. Then we scheduled the timing of implementing the new fundraising and volunteer initiatives.

## Statewide Domestic Violence Transitional Housing Agency

This agency wanted to increase foundation and corporate support, diversifying its fundraising revenues. Agency leaders built their foundation program through prospect research and staff training. And they initiated their corporate giving program using existing business relationships.

The development staff knew the differences between applying for foundation and government grants and their reporting requirements, but the program and finance staff did not. There was a lot of resistance on the part of non-development staff to the idea of increasing institutional funding. The program directors knew first-hand that their government contracts did not cover all their expenses. The finance staff didn't want to be tied up with rigorous financial reporting requirements that the agency was not reimbursed for.

So, we all sat down together and talked about needs. We talked about the need to cover administrative costs and realize a surplus so programs could grow. We talked about financial reporting requirements and what could and could not be matched with government funds. We talked about the pros and cons of further diversifying funding.

The development staff then went back and created a grants plan that pretty much met everyone's needs. They went back to the group with the plan, speaking to the previously voiced needs. They pointed out that their plan increased revenues for general operating costs with mostly simple reporting requirements, as long as program elements were implemented on time and outcomes tracked. The group responded by creating communication and reporting processes where no one department would be significantly taxed, and the pre- and post-grant information was available to everyone who needed it. To help motivate the rest of the non-development staff, the development director highlighted non-fundraising departmental contributions at staff meetings.

The next challenge was creating the corporate giving program. We decided to start with the existing business relationships the agency had and expand from there. So, I asked for a list of their vendors with annual payables. The development director identified which were already sponsoring and attending events at what levels. We created a more comprehensive and diversified menu of donation options so that any business could support the mission, no matter its size.

We thought that networking events would be of interest to the businesspeople. To encourage informal interaction, the networking meeting started with a meal and networking time. To move the discussion from business transactions to philanthropy, the agenda included a description of the mission in action and a client testimonial. The development staff then followed up with meeting attendees and asked them about their experiences.

Because the non-development staff felt heard by the development staff, their needs were met, and their contributions recognized, it was much easier to mobilize them to support the corporate giving program. Program staff eagerly made time to prepare, transport, and accompany clients to these meetings. Other key staff members were also invited to the meeting to network as well. The result was that key staff from all departments saw how participating in fundraising initiatives benefited them.

## Community Drug Prevention Agency

Because of their dire financial position, this agency needed to implement fundraising activities that produced almost immediate results. They also needed more people fundraising for them.

The executive director had to change the focus of the fundraising from one of asking the donor for money to one of asking for participation in mission fulfillment and growth. So, we created a case for support and integrated that message in all their individual appeals, grants, and special events.

We also changed the focus from gross income to net income and put all costs, direct and indirect, into the fundraising budgets. That way, the organization was not underestimating its fundraising costs. With total costs accounted for, it had a better idea of how many resources they needed to raise through each fundraising activity.

We also calculated their returns on investment for each activity. We created a development plan that focused on the agency's strengths and where the nonprofit was making the most money. The plan ended up with a strong focus on individual giving.

The next step was to get more people fundraising for them. Since they had a robust volunteer program and many volunteers, after the board, the first place we turned was the volunteer base. The case for support came in handy. The volunteer manager took the messaging from the case and incorporated it into the volunteer recruitment packets, training manuals, and volunteer recognition events. The volunteers would hear the same message multiple times at different points of contact. The board, staff, and volunteers were then on the same page in describing the agency to the community.

The organization was also in dire need of new low-cost fundraising and recordkeeping software. It had to streamline its recordkeeping systems so that the staff could accurately track revenues and expenses, and leadership could be aware of its financial position at all times. The new software would also help the bookkeeper realize efficiencies in monthly financial reconciliations.

## International Maternal Health Education Agency

To increase the unrestricted revenues this agency hoped for, this agency needed to build a robust fundraising infrastructure, including fundraising staff, a fundraising plan, donor connections, and a more advanced way to track donors and donations and generate reports. To garner more general operating monies, we focused our efforts on reaching individual and business donors.

The first step in this engagement was to create a case for support that gave the staff words to tell their story in a new way. This case could then be used as a basis for all of their fundraising messaging, no matter the audience.

Our next step was to create a development plan that leveraged the nonprofit's strengths within the limits of its organizational capacity. The plan was comprehensive, covering technology, communications, campaigns and appeals, staffing, and board involvement. The plan extended three years into the future, with additional fundraising staff recommendations based on their current staff structure. The agency did have someone who wrote grants, and they had hired a communications specialist.

Since individual donations are generally unrestricted and communications and fundraising endeavors can easily be integrated, our initial focus was on developing an individual-giving program. That program would start with social media and email campaigns and evolve to include major and planned gifts.

Then we worked on corporate outreach. This was a new way of funding for this nonprofit. We trained key staff in the principles and strategies of asking for business donations, highlighting the difference between the motivations behind why businesses, governments, foundations, and individuals give.

Program staff had expressed interest in learning about fundraising, too. Like the transitional housing agency, they knew all too well the limits of restricted funding. They wanted to help raise more unrestricted revenues if they could. So, we conducted a staff fundraising training. We talked about what fundraising was and wasn't, mission-driven efforts, how fundraising affected operations, and how the staff could participate without becoming fundraisers. It was gratifying to see how many of the staff participated.

## Bringing It Together

You want to mobilize your staff to raise the most money possible. To do that, focus on your mission. The best fundraisers are organizational ambassadors who talk about their agencies' missions and mission impact. Set specific, measurable, action-oriented, realistic, and time-bound goals and evaluate fundraising performance in relation to them. Set your staff up for financial success through your budgeting. Budget realistic revenues and expenses. Compare returns on investment. Budget for a surplus. Avoid the common pitfalls that hinder financial stability and growth. Evaluate total success, that is, mission fulfillment, financial performance, and strengthening important relationships. Paint the big picture, giving your fundraising staff a complete organizational picture. Development staff interact with all agency departments and the community. Help them do their jobs. And build strong teams. Integrate fundraising throughout your nonprofit. Then watch your financial and mission returns grow.

## Points to Remember

- Focus your fundraising staff on your mission. Fundraising activities that ooze the organization's mission, provide funds for the mission, and generate mission support are the ones that will be the most successful, financially and otherwise.

- Remember, what gets measured gets done. Make the goals you give your staff SMART. The SMARTer your goals, the more successful your staff will be in meeting them.

- Don't set your development staff up for fundraising and financial failure. Budget conservatively, accounting for total costs. Spread your risk by diversifying your revenue streams. Build in a surplus and put a portion of it aside.

- Retaining existing donors is just as important as acquiring new ones. Allocate staff time toward it. Improving your donor retention rate may be the most cost-effective and beneficial way you can realize increased revenues.

- Fundraising staff interact with program, finance, IT, marketing, communications, volunteer training and management, the board, and the community. They work most effectively when they are aware of any internal and external changes to your nonprofit.

## What's Next?

We've been talking about mobilizing your development staff. But just who are those staff? What do they do? When do you need to hire for different fundraising positions? How do you recruit, work with, and retain effective fundraising staff? You find answers in the next chapter.

Chapter Eight

# We're Hiring!

Y ou can implement The Sustainable High ROI Fundraising System no matter how big or small your agency is. By implementing the system, your nonprofit will grow, and you will need to add staff. Who you look for to staff your fundraising efforts depends on your skills, your agency's stage of growth, and what elements of your fundraising program you need help with.

This chapter addresses a new way to look at common development roles. We cover the different staff positions first, including when to consider hiring that specific staff position. We then describe how to work with a development director so that both you and the development director function optimally. We go on to discuss how to recruit and retain development professionals. Next, we look at common points of friction between executive directors and development directors. We end the chapter with tips on what to do if you are the sole fundraiser and have no development staff.

## Building Your Development Staff

You can hire full- or part-time fundraising staff or consultants, depending on your budget. Just know that experience is worth the price. An experienced development professional will bring efficiencies and know-how with them, getting more done in less time.

When you are looking for fundraising staff, look for personable people who have:

- Passion for your mission

- Integrity and engender trust

- Excellent interpersonal and social skills

- Excellent communication skills

- Determination, perseverance, and resilience

- Creative thinking and problem-solving skills

In your interview process, don't be bowled over by big numbers. Ask what those numbers represent—gross or net revenues. In addition to dollars raised, ask about donor acquisition and retention. And determine trends. You want to see if their results are consistent over time. We spoke about the importance of implementing smart fundraising and financial measures in **Chapter Seven**. The most important fundraising evaluation metrics and how to calculate them are listed in **Appendix B**.

## Development Director

If you don't have a fundraising background, you will want to hire a development director to help you bring in revenue. A development director is a fundraising generalist with skills and experience in a wide variety of revenue generation activities. A development director oversees all of your fundraising. Their duties include managing donor relationships, interacting with donors to encourage giving, writing and submitting grant proposals, seeking out sponsorships, and executing fundraising events. You need to hire a development director if your nonprofit maintains a varied revenue mix and you want to hire a generalist who knows a little about everything.

Specific duties for a development director may include:

- Creating the annual development plan and calendar

- Creating the development department and activity-specific budgets

- Identifying prospective individual, foundation, and corporate donors

- Researching donors
- Participating in donor networking opportunities
- Cultivating donor relationships
- Authoring and managing the annual appeal
- Asking individual donors for personal gifts
- Writing foundation and government grants
- Encouraging employee matching gifts
- Overseeing in-kind contributions
- Pursuing cause marketing relationships such as agreements to promote giving among customers or receive a percentage of sales
- Garnering event, program, and agency sponsorships
- Executing fundraising events including:
  - Securing an emcee, speakers, photographer, and videographer
  - Speechwriting
  - Preparing the mailing list, designing and sending invitations, managing registrations, collecting money, table seating, menu planning creating name tags, pursuing corporate sponsorships
  - Selling and gathering ads for an ad journal
  - Designing the ad journal
  - Securing necessary government licenses
  - Overseeing a live auction, silent auction, and 50/50 or other raffle
- Drafting memoranda of understanding and other agreements with donors
- Thanking donors
- Recording donations and interactions with donors
- Evaluating fundraising performance

- Sharing fundraising results
- Recruiting, training, managing, and evaluating fundraising volunteers
- Staffing the development committee
- Supervising and evaluating staff
- Implementing marketing and communications efforts
- Interacting with board members

Obviously, it's a big job, and the development director will need support. Just as obvious is the high skill level good development directors will bring with them. For top-notch talent, look for one with a certification as a fundraising executive.

Look to hire a development director when all the fundraising responsibilities become too much for you or you are inexperienced in fundraising. You always have the option of hiring part-time. When your budget is small, you may want to consider securing a development consultant who can create a case for support, outline a development plan, and provide you with the training you need to implement their plans.

You need a development director as soon as you can afford to add staff. Your objective is to progress in fulfilling your nonprofit's mission while raising the revenues to fund it within the time limits of performing your other job duties.

In addition to other giving vehicles, a good development director should be familiar with the planned giving

**Food for Thought**

For the highest return on investment and lowest opportunity costs, ensure your development director has access to good administrative support.

vehicles available to high-net-worth individuals such as simple bequests, charitable remainder trusts, annuities, donations of stock, donor-advised funds, and family foundations, to name a few. Often, development directors work with attorneys, accountants, and financial planners as fundraising volunteers when securing planned gifts. Do not expect development directors to be estate planning or tax experts, though. Expect them to work in concert with financial and estate planning professionals to maximize tax benefits.

When deciding what you want your development director to do precisely, consider your return on investment of them performing specific tasks versus an administrative assistant or event planner. Also, consider the opportunity costs of doing one activity instead of another. Ask yourself, "How can I get the most out of the limited time a development director has? Who is most skilled and will perform tasks more quickly? Who costs more—your development director, an assistant, or an event planner?"

Because the job is relationship intensive, you do not want to hire a consultant to be your development director. You want someone who is more permanent to your organization, solidifying your nonprofit's important donor relationships.

## Fundraising Assistant

A fundraising assistant provides administrative support to the development director and staff and participates in all fundraising activities, including donor relations, direct mailings, assembling grant packages, special events, and recordkeeping. Specific duties may include:

- General correspondence
- Meeting preparation
- Mailings
- Thank-you letters
- Event coordination
- Data entry
- Recordkeeping
- Running reports
- Prospect research

Whether you, the executive director, are the fundraiser or you have hired a development director, you will need some sort of administrative support to help in your fundraising efforts. In my experience, nonprofits underinvest in administrative support. A good administrative assistant, though, is worth the investment.

Although it may not be an assistant solely devoted to development, you need to hire a good administrative support person as your third hire. The investment is well worth the cost.

## Grant Writer

A grant writer prepares proposals by identifying opportunities and matching them to organizational needs, reviewing application guidelines, attending funder meetings, formatting information, writing drafts, obtaining approvals, and submitting requests. They have specific skills sets that are not common with other forms of fundraising, mainly because of the heavy emphasis on writing and formatting combined with building institutional donor relationships. Relationships with foundations, governmental agencies, and civic, religious, or community groups are identified and approached differently than individual donors. Institutional funders also tend to have more formal reporting requirements. A good grant writer will understand the art and science behind grant writing and the complexities in the field.

You can hire a grant writer as an employee or consultant. Be aware, though, that within grant writing, writing foundation grants and writing government grants require divergent skill sets. Government grants have political influences that foundation and community grants do not. Even if you hire a grant writer, you may still need a government grant consultant to advise you on pursuing government funding.

Specific job duties of a grant writer may include:

- Identifying potential funding opportunities
- Researching prospects
- Creating a grants calendar
- Authoring foundation, government, and community group proposals

- Coordinating program, finance, and administrative efforts around the requirements of specific funders

- Drafting program and grant budgets

- Assembling and mailing grant packages

- Generating thank-you letters

- Drafting grant reports to funders

- Drafting grant reports to department supervisors

- Recordkeeping

If grant writing is not your development director's strength or you do the fundraising and need to parcel out some of your duties, hiring a grant writer is a good option. Grant writing, along with events coordination, is easily definable and measurable. Just know that your grant writer will need your support, especially in coordinating their efforts with program and finance staff.

You need a grant writer when you become large enough to afford a development professional with specific grant writing skills. If you are experienced in fundraising and just need someone to write grants, you may wish to hire a grant writer before you hire a development director. Or, if you have a development director, but your fundraising program has grown so much that it needs help, you may wish to hire a grant writer. I have seen nonprofits with both scenarios.

## A New Development Staffing Paradigm

As your organization grows, instead of hiring traditional fundraising specialists, I recommend hiring higher-level fundraising generalists. In his book ***Personalized Philanthropy: Crash the Fundraising Matrix***, Steven Meyers calls these fundraisers enlightened generalists. Enlighted generalists are fundraisers who are trained and experienced in all avenues donors use to bestow gifts. They do not specialize in any one method. Build a team with similar skills and complementary strengths around your donors' needs, not your fundraising methods.

When you are fully staffed, your organization will look something like this:

## Sample Development Organization Chart

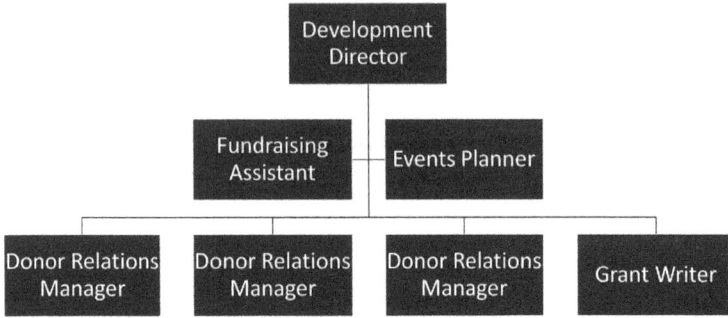

And your management matrix will look something like this:

## How to Build Your Development Staff

| | Researching | Cultivating | Asking | Stewarding |
|---|---|---|---|---|
| Development Director | Individual Donor Group 1 | | | |
| Donor Relations Manager 1 | Individual Donor Group 2 | | | |
| Donor Relations Manager 2 | Individual Donor Group 3 | | | |
| Donor Relations Manager 3 | Individual Donor Group 3 | | | |
| Grant Writer | Foundation and Government Funders | | | |

By centering your efforts around building relationships, you ensure that your development staff is taking care of total donor needs. For example, in a traditional office, I have seen potentially big donors asked for small gifts or two different types of fundraisers approaching donors with conflicting asks. Structuring your fundraising staff around the donor avoids embarrassing situations like these, lessening your risk of losing donors and their gifts.

Most small to mid-sized nonprofits automatically default to hiring a generalist. But then they build toward specialization, not realizing the focus of their fundraising program moves from centering around donor relationships to implementing processes. An emphasis on specialized skills silos your staff and creates a disjointed donor experience. When staff are siloed, communication and teamwork can suffer. I see this happen often at larger organizations.

## Traditional Development Offices

|  | Annual Appeal | Special Events | Major Giving | Planned Giving | Corporate Giving |
|---|---|---|---|---|---|
| Donor 1 |  |  |  |  |  |
| Donor 2 |  |  |  |  |  |
| Donor 3 |  |  |  |  |  |
| Donor 4 |  |  |  |  |  |
| Donor 5 |  |  |  |  |  |
| Donor 6 |  |  |  |  |  |
| Donor 7 |  |  |  |  |  |

Compare the two matrices and notice how the first requires hiring less people with more skill and expertise. Although your individual salary costs may be more, your overall salary costs are lower. That's because you are using resources more efficiently. Putting the onus on generalist fundraisers to meet

### Food for Thought

Know that experience is worth the price. An experienced development professional will bring efficiencies and know-how with them, getting more done in less time.

total donor needs enables you to build relationships with more donors with less resource investment. And providing professional development opportunities to sharpen skills cost less than hiring for a new position.

Which means that you need top notch fundraiser recruitment and retention strategies. We talk about attracting and retaining talent later in the chapter.

## Differences Between Traditional Development Offices and the New Paradigm

| Traditional Development Office | New Paradigm |
| --- | --- |
| Employs all fundraising methods | Employs all fundraising methods |
| Fundraiser involved with one fundraising method | Fundraiser involved with multiple fundraising methods |
| Donor involved with multiple fundraising staff | Donor involved with one fundraiser |
| Requires hiring multiple specialized fundraising staff | Requires hiring fundraising generalists |
| Emphasizes implementing correct fundraising methods and processes | Emphasizes building donor relationships |

## Traditional Fundraising Roles

If you build toward specialization, you end up a siloed staff that with the following responsibilities.

### Special Events Coordinator

Fundraising event coordination has two aspects to it: event planning and fundraising. A special events coordinator plans, organizes, promotes, and executes your agency's fundraising events. They are also responsible for making money through the events. So they will be involved not only with individual donors who attend the event, but also corporate donors who sponsor the event.

### Major Gifts Officer

A major gifts officer develops strategies to realize big gifts through the cultivation, solicitation, and stewardship of individual donors. They are usually supervised by a development director and brought on board once a nonprofit has enough individual donors to warrant the expense. Because they deal with higher-net-worth individuals, they are usually paid more than grant writers and event coordinators.

## Planned Giving Officer

A planned giving officer needs to be familiar with the gift planning vehicles available to high-net-worth individuals, such as simple bequests, charitable remainder trusts, annuities, donations of stock, donor-advised funds, and family foundations, to name a few. They often have law or accounting degrees or have training to learn the complexities of gift planning. They work closely with the donor's advisors to maximize financial and tax benefits for the donor and the donor's heirs.

## Director of Foundation and Corporate Relations

If the grant writing is split into government and foundation grant writing, sometimes a nonprofit hires a director of foundation and corporate relations. This person is responsible for all the foundation grant writing and for developing relationships with the businesses that will support your special events and other corporate initiatives.

## Director of Corporate Relations

Sometimes, there is a director of corporate relations. A position like this can usually be found alongside a director of foundations. The director of corporate relations is responsible for all business relationships, whether the business gives through grants, outright monetary gifts, employee matching gifts, gifts in kind, sponsorships, discounts, employee volunteers, percentage of sales, promotion, or any other vehicle.

## Capital Campaign Manager

A capital campaign manager specializes in capital campaigns. This person is often hired as a consultant, working with your development staff in asking for special large-project support. Capital campaigns encompass all types of fundraising—individual, grant, and business support.

A good capital campaign consultant will conduct a thorough feasibility study, including collecting and analyzing information on your nonprofit's economic, technical, legal, and scheduling considerations to assess the likelihood of successful campaign completion.

You hire a capital campaign manager when you need to raise money for large projects, such as a building purchase or renovation, buying a substantial piece of equipment, or establishing an endowment.

## Executive Director-Development Staff Fundraising Responsibilities

Although your fundraising staff are responsible for implementing specific fundraising activities, you also bear some responsibility for how well your development staff performs. You work in tandem as a team. You, the executive director, set the tone, providing the environment your development staff operate in to raise the financial support needed for the agency to thrive and grow. Both of you deal with the external environment. Both are dependent on one another to ensure success. Both engage in some of the same tasks, just at different levels, such as planning, budgeting, and evaluating. How do you assign responsibilities so that together you produce the best financial results?

### Fundraising Responsibilities to Delegate

Although you and your board are responsible for the overall planning, particularly through creating a strategic plan, your development director is responsible for creating the annual development plan you oversee. A development plan is based on your nonprofit's mission and is focused on your agency's vision. It includes all aspects of the development process, including technology, communications, fundraising methods, staffing, and board involvement.

In the same vein, whereas you are responsible for creating organizational budgets, your development director creates a departmental and individual budget for each fundraising activity. The budgeting process will involve some back and forth, and you bear ultimate responsibility, but budgeting for day-to-day fundraising needs is something you can delegate.

You can also delegate the identification of new prospects, researching donors, data entry, and database management, as well as a fair amount of donor cultivation, solicitation, and stewardship. As the leader of the organization, you can't delegate it all, though. Major donors will want to meet with you. You can leave the logistics to your fundraising staff. However, you will still need to interact with important donors.

Same with evaluating fundraising performance. You can delegate the day-to-day and activity assessments to your staff, but you need to be on top of financial performance. When I was an executive director, I accomplished this level of oversight through daily monitoring of our financial position and revenue streams.

## Fundraising Responsibilities to Keep

There is no doubt about it. If your development staff are doing their jobs, they will spend a lot of time developing and nurturing relationships in the community. As such, they are keenly aware of your nonprofit's reputation in the general community. Tap into this knowledge so you can build an organization that is responsive to community needs, as well as those of clients. As the organization's day-to-day leader, you are the most significant influence on your nonprofit's culture. Creating a healthy culture is not something you can delegate. Tap into your development staff's experience with the external environment to inform you of the kind of culture the community will best respond to.

With so many operational issues needing your attention, it is easy to rely on your fundraising staff to be the face of your agency. Don't totally let them. Take your responsibility as the chief organizational representative and work *with* your development staff in building meaningful donor relationships. Meet with major donors with your development staff. You can leave the solicitation to the staff, but your presence as agency head is crucial.

In addition, you cannot delegate being the main staff liaison to the board. Work with the development director to involve your board in fundraising but don't abdicate your responsibility. It is vital that you set an example for and teach your board how to fundraise. We talked about engaging your board in fundraising in **Chapter Six**.

## Factors that Affect Fundraising Performance

A good fundraiser may or may not perform well for you because many factors that are out of their control influence their results. For example, community interest in your mission—there may or may not be a plethora of people out there who are interested in supporting your nonprofit's mission. Which is one reason why before conducting a capital campaign, you perform a feasibility study. I know that you think your nonprofit's mission is of the utmost importance, and once people hear about all the good your agency does, they will want to support you. It doesn't work that way, though. All nonprofits have important missions and can cite good work. You need to stand out from the crowd. We talk at length about how to get your community's attention and financial support in **Chapter Nine**.

Your agency history also affects how much money can be raised. For example, if you've struggled to raise twenty-five thousand dollars over the years, chances that you will raise a hundred thousand dollars this year are pretty slim. You just don't have the infrastructure in place to raise all that money. You need to build first. Have the policies, processes, and procedures in place that will help your fundraiser raise the amount of funds you hope for. Set reasonable expectations for performance and provide a culture where development professionals can thrive. Don't leave the fundraising all up to the development staff. Take a team approach, building on your role as executive director.

The larger economy also affects how much is reasonable to raise. If a recession hits, chances are good that individual donations will decrease. If the stock market slides, foundation corpuses may not be worth as much, causing them to limit the amount of money they give out. If there are negative industry shifts within your business community, you may not get the corporate contributions you are used to. If the unemployment rate is high, tax receipts will probably suffer, leading to government budget cuts or reallocations. Any or all of your revenue streams are, to some extent, dependent on the economy.

Because of all these outside influences, you may periodically conduct a thorough evaluation of your agency's fundraising strengths and weaknesses to see how you can counteract any negative influences affecting your organization's fundraising performance. We talked at length about assessing your fundraising strengths and gaps in **Chapter Four**.

## Needed Fundraising Skills

To fundraise effectively, the number one proficiency to hone is your and your development staff's relationship-building abilities. If you can build relationships, you can successfully raise money.

You also need to hone communication skills. Oral communication skills are important in face-to-face interactions. Writing skills are a must for grant writing. There are a variety of workshops and training opportunities available to improve oral and written communication skills.

Planning skills are important, too, especially when implementing fundraising events. I make lists, adding new tasks as they come up and deleting tasks as I complete them.

Time management skills are essential if you have a large workload, which most of us do. I usually find trainings in time management through corporate training firms.

Negotiating skills are likewise a must. Sales courses help develop competency in this area.

Budgeting expertise is also extremely helpful, especially if you are responsible for grant budgets, event finances, or overall fundraising performance. Exceeding revenue projections and keeping costs down are top concerns of board members.

Knowing how to measure results, evaluate your data, and which metrics are important competencies are worth developing, too. As I've said before, what gets measured gets done. And it's hard to argue with objective data.

Read a book, attend a workshop, take a class, join a professional association, or find a mentor. Tackle one skill at a time until you are a master.

## Working with Development Professionals

Hopefully, you are working with professionals who carry a passion for your nonprofit's mission, are good relationship builders, maintain a donor-centric customer service approach, and abide by industry standards. The Association for Fundraising Professionals and the Grant Professionals Association require their members to abide by specific ethical standards. You're off to a good start if your fundraiser belongs to one or both of those groups.

Some fundraisers, much to my chagrin, do not perform well or are unethical. How do you find the best prospects to work with, staff or consultant? And once you've found someone good who you work well with, how do you keep them?

### Consultants

The role of a consultant is to provide opinions, analyses, and recommendations based on their expertise. They have an objective pair of eyes, providing strategies to prevent problems and improve performance. Fundraising consultants may have skills in developing annual campaigns, writing grants, implementing special events, asking for corporate donations, building major gift programs, conducting capital campaigns, recommending donor management systems, or advising in general nonprofit organization administration. Their main goal is to achieve desired fundraising objectives and targets. They can be individuals or employees of a firm. The ideal consultant will have previous fundraising experience, excellent communication skills, strong organizational skills, and proven experience in budgeting and managing money.

The first step to finding a good consultant is to determine your nonprofit's needs and goals. As we pointed out in **Chapter Four**, your nonprofit is unique in many ways. You want to make sure that you select someone who can work within your agency's specific structure and culture.

Do your research. Understand the services the consultant offers. Assess their history in the type of project you need to be done. There are many types of fundraising consultants who can focus on different types of fundraising activities or their separate elements. Use your network to ask for recommendations.

Interview several firms. Ask about their values. Evaluate their expertise. Ascertain how their clients are better off at the end and after the engagement. Ask them what makes their approach unique. Assess workstyle. Question them about their work processes and whether they will be working alone or with others. As they will be dealing with proprietary information, ask how they will ensure confidentiality. Determine their availability to you. Understand the engagement, fees, and payment process. And ask how many other engagements they will manage at one time.

If you are interested in working with them, request a proposal and ask for references.

## Staff

### Food for Thought

The average tenure for a development director is fourteen months. Do what you can to stop that revolving door.

The average tenure for a fundraising professional is fourteen months. According to a recent study by the Association of Fundraising Professionals, half of the fundraisers surveyed reported that they intend to leave their jobs in the next two years.

And the results are costly. If you lose your development director, you have no one to do the fundraising until you find a replacement. Or you overtax existing staff. Your fundraising institutional knowledge goes out the door. Donor recruitment, cultivation, and stewardship don't get done. Relationships suffer. As a result, you lose donors. Revenues suffer. Not only do revenues decrease, costs increase. To find a new development director, you have immediate staff recruitment and training costs. Then you have donor acquisition costs, which are often six times more than your donor retention costs. You want to do everything in your power to stop that revolving door.

Development professionals leave their jobs and look for new ones because:

1. They don't feel supported.

2. The culture is toxic.

3. There is little or no organizational infrastructure to facilitate philanthropy.

We talk about you how to can best support them later in this chapter. We spoke to creating healthy fundraising cultures in **Chapters Six** and **Seven**. We explain how to build a robust fundraising infrastructure that excites your board, staff, and community throughout this book.

*Attracting Talent*

Development professionals want to work for nonprofits that will pay them fairly, set realistic performance expectations, and support their position. They don't want to work in a silo. Nor do they want to be seen as the financial savior.

To attract high-quality candidates, be responsive to requests for information. Evaluate whether you share goals. Provide for personal and professional development. Give them flexibility in their schedules. Get your board excited about fundraising, as we discussed in **Chapter Six**. Create a fundraising culture, as we addressed in **Chapter Seven**. And focus on the needs of your community, as we delve into in **Chapter Nine**.

To find development professionals, go where they are. You may want to attend industry meetings, conferences, or other gatherings, maybe even sponsor a professional development opportunity. Try approaching professional associations related to the type of fundraising professional you are looking for, such as the Association of Fundraising Professionals and Grant Professionals Association. You can also try your state's affiliate of the National Council on Nonprofits. Every state has one.

## Keeping Talent

You want your staff to be productive, feel satisfied in their work, strive for excellence, work as a team, and take responsibility for their jobs. You want to empower them to reach their potential.

Most workers strive to succeed. They want to do a good job. Most often, people tend to perform poorly because of an obstacle impeding their performance. Perhaps they weren't trained properly, misunderstood instructions, received unclear direction, were not given a deadline, or simply had too much to do. Get rid of these hindrances. Write accurate job descriptions, provide up-to-date employee policies and procedures, implement a standard agency orientation, develop job-specific training programs, give employees an introductory period to learn their jobs, create a mentorship program, and have new employees shadow more experienced staff. And provide incentives for doing a good job.

### External Motivators

External motivators are used all the time in the for-profit world. One external motivator is linking raises and bonuses to performance, i.e., giving merit bonuses rather than cost-of-living increases. You can also tie raises to overall agency financial success. When the organization realizes a net surplus, some of the proceeds are distributed to staff. Or combine the two.

Another external motivator is praise. When you give praise, don't just give general "good job" praise. Give specific thanks for a particular accomplishment. For example, "Thank you for speaking with Mr. Jones. He is an important community leader with a lot of influence. By introducing him to the work of our nonprofit, you paved the way for us to have lunch together. Now he's interested in donating to our cause and getting some of his contacts involved, too." Specific praise tells an employee you are aware of their actions and appreciate their good work. And they know they made a valuable contribution to the agency.

Internal Motivators

While external motivators work, internal motivators work even better. Evidence of internal workplace motivation means that employees can generate their own sense of value and job satisfaction. Don't get me wrong—outside input is still important. People want to feel acknowledged and appreciated. External motivators are still important. But internal motivators don't cost money and are far more effective.

One way to motivate development staff is to give them financial and mission goals without specifying how they should reach them. Let them figure it out and tell you what works best for them and the organization. Then monitor progress, giving praise each time a milestone is reached. Your staff will feel they have made a contribution and that their contribution is valued. As a result, they become vested in the process. For best results, make the goals as specific as possible. Let your fundraisers define the individual methods that they will use to meet those goals. Let them define how they can best contribute.

Of course, to do this, you must have a strong, consistent vision, be willing to share your goals, create a culture that encourages healthy discussion, and give up some control. By doing so, you create a shared leadership model. Shared leadership promotes autonomy, which generates even more internal motivation and job satisfaction.

*Foster Talent*

Professional development is not a perk. It's a necessity. You want your development staff to grow and develop so they realize efficiencies in their work and pick up advanced fundraising skills to raise more money. Provide professional memberships to your staff. Budget for them. Give your staff time to attend meetings. There they can network with other fundraisers who can help them solve a vexing problem, give them that next great fundraising idea, or support them in their work. They may even be able to find a mentor who can help them navigate the fundraising process.

Also, allow time for training. Encourage your staff to pursue professional certifications. Pay for industry workshops and conferences, Reimburse tuition for college and university classes. You need to set monetary limits, for sure. Just budget something, even if it is only time to attend. The results more than make up for the costs.

*Encourage Teamwork*

Non-fundraising staff make sure that the organization meets its client objectives, the finances are on the up and up, and operations run efficiently—all of which influence how much money can be raised. Fundraising staff must understand the totality of what needs to get done. Fundraising staff often work in a silo. More often than not, there is only one fundraising staff person whose job is different from any other job in the organization. Which means they often do not fully appreciate the demands of other staff. In the same vein, non-fundraising staff often haven't a clue as to what a fundraiser does. Non-fundraising staff may only see the fun parts of development, like lunch meetings and evening parties.

To counteract misconceptions, give your staff a glimpse of what other staff are dealing with. Hold team meetings, encourage cross-department friendships, and create communication, reporting, and fidelity systems that promote teamwork. For example, I have seen program staff wince at the development director bringing in so much money because it caused so much more work for them. Usually, that was because the front lines staff, fundraising staff, and finance staff had not discussed a fundraising plan that worked within their respective capacities.

Make sure your fundraiser doesn't become a lone ranger or think that everyone thinks the more money they bring in, the better. They have to coordinate their work with non-fundraising staff. Make sure you create opportunities for all staff to appreciate and understand the role and capacity of all other staff.

## Be Ethical

It is unethical in the field to pay fund-raisers a percentage of funds raised. I know a fair amount of salespeople are paid on a commission basis. In those cases, the companies' profits benefit

### Warning!

It is unethical in the field to pay fundraisers on a percentage basis. Stay away from fundraisers willing to accept commissions.

the private business owner, not the public. When the money goes for the inurement of the public, different standards apply. Payment of a percentage of fees given for the public good is not fair to all parties involved. Because there are so many organizational factors out of their control—for example, the percentage of board giving, the financial position of the agency, or political influences affecting donor decisions—the fundraiser deserves to be paid whether a donation goes through or not. And the agency shouldn't have to pay a big chunk of revenues to fundraisers because of a big donation. Number one, that means money is not going toward the mission but is going to an individual. Nonprofits have a legal responsibility to use public funds for public inurement, not private inurement. Number two, the compensation may be above what the fundraiser is worth. Moreover, that's not fair to the donor who donates to a cause, not a paycheck. I know some people do it. Stay away from these people; it is unethical to pay fundraisers on a commission basis.

## The Executive Director-Development Director Relationship

Often, the executive director-development director relationship is somewhat conflictual. This is not surprising as most nonprofit executive directors rise up through the program or, less often, the financial ranks of an agency. This means that most often, the development director and executive director have different perspectives on ensuring the agency's financial health. Typical points of conflict between executive directors and development directors include situations when dealing with the public, managing board relationships, spending, and delegating fundraising tasks.

### The Face of the Agency

Both executive directors and development directors interact with the community and are public figures. Both of you are building and nurturing relationships, building trust between you and who you are connecting with. Because of the strength of the relationship, sometimes it happens that a donor's loyalty moves from the organization to the individual. If you're not careful, the development director can become the face of the agency to important constituencies. It can also happen that you become so involved in whatever operational issues you are dealing it can overshadow your time with the community. Or the development director does not share complete information with you. Information is power. And then you get into a power struggle.

To prevent your development director from becoming the face of the agency, it's crucial for you to attend important donor meetings and functions and meet regularly with your development director in both office and community settings. You want to see them in action and know that you are fully informed about the development director's relationships. This is why, too, that your development director should report directly to you.

It is vital that you clearly define your level of involvement with donors early on and that you both understand how the lines of communication with important constituencies will flow. I know it can be hard, but you need to find the time to attend to fundraising matters and subtly reinforce the balance of power between you and your development director.

## Board Relations

Because the board leadership in fundraising is crucial (we talked about your board and fundraising in **Chapter Six**), your development director will interact with the board, if only to thank them for their donations. It is easy for a board member to form a relationship with the development director apart from you. Which is okay, as long as the board member does not discuss board business with the development director or triangle you into any conflict between the two. Dealing with the board is hard enough. You want to avoid as many complexities to your relationship with board members as you can.

Like with donor relationships, you must define roles and lines of communication up front to both your development director and the board. You may even want to develop a board-staff relationship policy that is included in board and staff recruitment materials, board manuals, and employee handbooks. And then stick to the policy.

## Resource Investment

As an executive director, you are hopefully closely managing costs and spending. Not only do you want to avoid overspending, but you also have to report on financial performance to your board, and they may question costs.

If net income is negative, most board members, operations officers, and finance directors think of cutting costs first. In contrast, from a fundraising perspective, you may need to *spend* more money. Fundraisers think an investment in development is what is needed when revenues are not meeting expectations. Obviously, you shouldn't spend money you don't have. But underinvestment in fundraising leads to poor financial results. And, if you want to keep your development director, you want them to have the support they need to do their job. You want to stop the fourteen-month revolving door.

It all comes down to planning and budgeting. It takes money to make money. For example, you need to identify, recruit, cultivate, and solicit donors before realizing their donations. You need basic infrastructure to track and report on the contributions and donor relationships you build. At the least, you need to send out tax receipts to donors at the end of the year. So, your development director is asking you to spend first while everyone else wants you to cut costs.

You must plan and budget to invest in fundraising to realize the kind of financial success you want. And you have to communicate your plans throughout the organization so that everyone knows what to expect. Which means you engage in strategic planning. And that your development director creates the development plan based on the strategic plan. And that you and your development director budget well, both on the macro and micro level. And manage the budgets so that you do, in fact, realize positive net income. That's a goal everyone buys into. We talked about strategic budgeting in **Chapter Seven**.

## Transactional and Relational Processes

### Clarifying Point

Fundraising is not about the money. It is about building relationships with people motivated by your nonprofit's mission and showing them how they can participate in fulfilling that mission through a financial donation.

Fundraising can be looked at as a series of transactions. You ask for money, the donor gives a gift, the gift is recorded, the donor gets a thank-you letter with the standard tax-deductible language (except for donations from donor-advised funds). That's the process your finance officer sees, and probably your chief operating officer, too. Sometimes even board members. After all, it's all about getting the money, isn't it?

*No.* It's *not* all about getting the money. It's about building a relationship with people motivated by your nonprofit's mission and showing them how they can participate in fulfilling that mission through a financial donation.

This difference in understanding what fundraising is and isn't leads to conflicting thoughts on what job tasks are required to meet the overall financial goal. One focuses on the process of realizing a donation. The other emphasizes the importance of building strong connections with donors. So, the pressure is on you to make the transactions happen, and your fundraiser is talking about footing an expensive lunch meeting. Think about the implications of these differences in how your development director wants to write the annual appeal, annual report, website content, or promotional materials. If you and your development director are not on the same page, it's a recipe for frustration.

### Living with the Divergence

Because of the inherent tension between the perspectives of an executive director and development director and the pressures you both face, as a result, you need to be in constant communication and establish mutual trust. Let your development director know what you want and expect from the relationship. In turn, ask your development director what they want and expect. And make it easy for your development director to trust you. Treat them as the professionals they are. Understand how their approaches are different than yours. Expect differences and treat disagreements as part of the necessary course of business. Respect their opinions. Let them know that you appreciate their efforts. Listen to their fears and frustrations. They are likely to respond in kind.

## When *You* Are the Development Department

If you are the only staff in your nonprofit dedicated to fundraising, I feel for you. As an executive director, your plate is full tending to existing and emergent issues. If you have a background in fundraising, it's bad enough. If you don't, the task is next to impossible. In either case, you will need help. Where do you go for support?

Your board is where you start. Board members may think fundraising is your job, not theirs, but the truth is fundraising is *everyone's* job. To fulfill the mission, you need money, and to get money, your need to fulfill the mission. They go hand in hand. The mission and money are so dependent on each other that they cannot be separated. Your board needs to realize that fact. We discussed how to engage your board in fundraising in **Chapter Six**.

At the same time, approach your non-fundraising staff if you have them. Create an organizational culture where your staff become mission ambassadors for your agency, thus supporting your fundraising efforts. We talked about mobilizing your staff in **Chapter Seven**.

You also need to approach your community. Reach out and recruit volunteers to fundraise for you. Create a development committee that includes board members. Of course, this means you need to excite your community to be involved with your organization. I present a deep dive into how to excite your community in **Chapter Nine**. And you *will* need to excite your community. You need as many hands on deck as you can handle.

If you are working with volunteers, you will need to choose structured fundraising methods to fit their needs. Perhaps a peer-to-peer campaign, phone-a-thon, or face-to-face solicitations. Of course, this means you need to train and onboard your volunteers correctly. Volunteers, like staff, appreciate and respond to structure. They need things like job descriptions, training manuals, and performance evaluations. Your materials may not be as formal as with your employees, but you need them nonetheless. And you need to give your volunteers feedback on their performance. Acknowledge and validate their contributions and correct them when they make mistakes. Publicly and privately thank and recognize them for their gifts of time and talent. Create a leadership structure they can move into as they seek more challenges.

Remember, you've got this. The board hired you for a reason. Breathe. Delegate what you can. Take time for yourself. And follow the suggestions for moving forward we outlined in **Chapter Two**.

## Bringing It Together

Consider staffing your development department with fundraising generalists and administrative and event planning specialists. Foster your development department's personal and professional growth. Budget for professional development, even if you can only afford to give time. Use the finely chiseled skills to garner the most amount of money possible. Delegate the day-to-day fundraising responsibilities to your development director while keeping your strategic planning, major donor cultivation, culture creation, and board liaison roles. Know that your fundraisers face many obstacles that are out of their control, including community interest in your nonprofit's mission, agency history and capacity, and the overall economy. Work with development professionals who exhibit a passion for your agency's mission, are good relationship builders, utilize a donor-centric customer service approach, and abide by industry standards. To attract good staff, pay them fairly, set realistic expectations, and provide support for them. To keep them, provide external motivators. Give specific praise liberally. Do not pay your fundraisers on a commission basis; instead, structure the work and environment to foster internal motivators.

You and your development director may clash on issues relating to the face of the agency, how to work with the board, spending on fundraising endeavors, and how to achieve the best financial results.

Respect and understand their viewpoint. Treat them as the professional they are. Expect conflict. Address the conflict before it happens, sharing early on what you both want and expect from the relationship.

If you are the sole staff fundraiser, engage your board in fundraising (see **Chapter Six**). Mobilize all agency staff to become agency mission ambassadors (see **Chapter Seven**). And recruit fundraising volunteers from your community. Excite your community in supporting your agency (see **Chapter Nine**).

## Points to Remember

- Hire a development director first. Then add a grant writer. When your nonprofit is large enough, hire fundraising enlightened generalists. Always ensure your development staff members have adequate administrative support.

- Provide performance incentives for fundraising staff but be ethical about it. Remember, commission-based pay is considered unethical in the field. Instead, establish work processes and conditions that foster the expansion of internal motivators.

- Address conflict with your development director before it begins. Discuss early on both of your wants and expectations for the position.

- If you *are* the fundraising department, leverage your time and efforts by engaging your board in fundraising, mobilizing other staff, and exciting your community.

## What's Next?

Now that we know what development professionals' tasks are, it's time to go out into the community, interact with it, and recruit new donors. The next chapter covers what it takes to excite your community about your cause and get it to support your agency, financially and otherwise. You will see how to create visibility and stand out in the nonprofit crowd, meet donor goals, and develop a strong, successful organizational image. You will also explore how to invite new donors into your donor family.

## Chapter Nine

# Exciting Your Community

Most fundraising interventions miss the critical step of exciting the community and why it's essential. In this step, you capitalize on and influence community perceptions of your nonprofit so that you attract more community financial and mission backing.

You prepare to excite your community as you mobilize your staff and engage your board in fundraising. You want the infectious fundraising culture you have created through your staff and board to infiltrate your community. Your goal is to raise your nonprofit's profile to draw people to your cause and financially support your agency.

Results you can expect after implementing this step:

- More awareness of your nonprofit in the community
- Unified, consistent messaging that rallies the public to support your mission
- More advocates for your cause
- Increased financial support

## Judiciously Interact with Your Community

If you want to recruit more volunteers, donors, good board members, motivated staff, and advocates for your cause, you want the community to get excited about being involved with your nonprofit. The question to ponder is, "How can I position my nonprofit so that I find good people eager to help meet my agency's mission?"

## The Competition for Funds

Approximately 1.5 million United States nonprofits are vying for the attention necessary to raise the money they need. Many nonprofits struggle to be noticed in the fray. How do you get your agency to stand out in the crowd? How does your organization gain the visibility it needs to generate the stronger community support you desire? How does your nonprofit become so well known that it is a household word and people naturally think of supporting it?

Whenever you are looking to broaden community support and find new supporters, probe a little. Ask the questions:

- Do our fundraising efforts improve our agency's brand?

- Is our agency visible to our potential supporters?

- How inviting is the experience to join us?

## Be a Mission Hawk

If you want to stay within the purposes of your Articles of Incorporation, communicate to the community exactly what you stand for, and leverage your fundraising efforts, you need to be a mission hawk, *especially* when it comes to fundraising. You don't want your nonprofit to be known as the one always with its hand out asking for donations. Rather, you want to be known as the nonprofit in town that makes a tremendous impact, no matter what size the donation you receive. And to do that, you need your focus to be on your agency's mission. Always.

## Target Specific Donor Groups

Nonprofits crave community visibility. Most of them complain they are their community's best-kept secret.

When nonprofits talk about their efforts to gain visibility, most of them think about getting more media coverage, doing some advertising, or redesigning their website. While press releases, TV spots, radio interviews, flyers in stores, and logos on buses do raise a nonprofit's visibility, it's general visibility that they're raising. And while that's all well and good, and you do need some of it, those are not the most effective methods to raise strong support for your cause. Because you're not trying to reach everyone. You're trying to reach those people that have a penchant for what you do.

Attracting donors takes time and effort. And in the nonprofit world, with so much to do, time is hard to come by. There is so much to do with not enough time that you need to make every moment count. To squeeze the best results out of every effort, you must use the least resources for the most gain. And, with the limited resources most nonprofits operate with, you want to use those resources to get as much value as you can. You don't want to spend money looking for just anyone to support you. You are looking to expend resources such that they attract as many new donors as possible.

### Food for Thought

For a higher return on investment, expend resources not to reach everyone but to reach those who have a propensity for your mission.

Target the donors who will be most passionate about your mission and have the means to support it. And by target, I mean to define your donor groups as precisely as you can in terms of age, ethnicity, gender, education, income, likes, and preferences. The more narrowly defined your target group, the more likely you will realize success.

Why target smaller, distinct groups instead of going after everyone? Say you want to fish for flounder. You could go out with a boat, cast a wide net, and get a lot of fish, a few of which are flounder. Or, you could go where flounders tend to congregate, cast a small net, get fewer fish but a lot of which are flounder. In the first scenario, you expend a lot of resources to get a few of what you want. In the second, you don't end up with as many individual fish, but you get a whole lot more of what you want.

If you are trying to realize revenue as soon as possible, target people interested in your mission, particularly those with the capacity to make large gifts.

If you can wait for a big donation and have the time to nurture a relationship, go after high-net-worth donors who don't yet have affinity for your mission but could if you spent time and resources educating them. Know, though, that you will need a big hook to interest them. For example, some sort of lavish social event. In that case, realize that the primary goal of your event is not to raise money through the event. Instead, the primary goal of the event is to start a relationship with wealthy individuals. You can follow up with them after the event and develop their proclivity to your mission. Your donor relationship manager, an enlightened generalist, can talk intelligently about how to structure large gifts so that both your nonprofit and the donor maximize benefits.

People who are passionate for your cause will likely give you more than money. Like a good word when talking to their friends and family. Or volunteer time to help you run your programs or recruit other donors and volunteers. Or in-kind donations so that your costs are reduced. And the fact is that most people don't give large donations without a relationship in which to do it. The first phase to acquire new donors is to identify them. The second phase is to develop a relationship with them. Then, when the timing is right, you ask for money.

The best way for your agency to get more community financial support is for your message to come from the community itself. In other words, be the buzz. Reach a core group of supporters and, like a bullseye, let them reach the next ring out. And those people the ring after that. Imagine what that would do for your return on investment!

### Define Your Target Markets

A target market is a set of people who have something in common with one another. They share similar needs or characteristics, usually demographic characteristics, values, preferences, or behaviors. The more defined your target group, the easier it is to speak directly to them and allocate resources to have the biggest effect. With donors, you target people interested in your cause, connection to your nonprofit, and means to give financially.

Clients, board members, donors, staff, volunteers, advocates, and community leaders are the most critical constituencies for your nonprofit to reach. Each of these groups plays a vital role in advancing your agency's mission. Yet, each of these groups has its own set of demographic characteristics, likes, dislikes, values, places they hang out, and preferred methods of communication. Which means that each constituency needs its own outreach strategy. And its own value proposition.

*Research Your Target Groups*

Who are your nonprofit's most ardent supporters? What are their characteristics? What do they read? What groups are they part of? How do they communicate with one another? How do they spend their leisure time? What do they spend their money on? What is important to them? What are their values?

These are the types of questions you need to be asking your supporters. The answers to these questions will tell you where to find and communicate about what to people interested in supporting you. You need to know your supporters, inside and out. Start where you are with what you have. From there, branch out. And grow your base. You don't want to spend a lot of money not getting what you want. You are looking to expend resources so they generate the most support possible. You need to target your efforts.

Remember the old adage, "different strokes for different folks?" Well, it holds true in marketing.

To find out about your potential individual donors, research them. To learn their group values, beliefs, likes, and preferences, you might visit the Center for Generational Kinetics and analyze its research. Or you might start a conversation and interact with the people you want to reach, then write down your observations. Or you might conduct a survey or convene a focus group.

To learn about prospective foundation donors, study their IRS Form 990s and giving trends. Visit their websites. Study their application guidelines. Read their reports, white papers, and press releases. It's all public information.

You can study potential corporate donors by reviewing information on their website and in their corporate reports and company press releases. You might also want to become more proficient in understanding their issues and speaking their language by reading business journals and economic reports.

If you are researching potential government funders, visit their websites, see what they do and what they fund. Read the results of any community studies they have conducted. You also have legislation, rules, and regulations ad nauseam you can read.

When you get information about your donor groups, hear what they say, not what you want them to say. Listen to them. Find a way to loop back with them and confirm your perceptions. Take the evidence you end up with and use it to fashion your approach and subsequent communications to them. To get those communications just right, base your efforts on the objective data they have provided.

### Define the Benefits to Your Target Groups

A value proposition is a statement of the benefits a supporter will receive by being involved with your agency. A value proposition helps potential supporters see how the implementation of your nonprofit's mission is of value to them and why your nonprofit is worth getting involved in within their sea of options.

A well-written value proposition will explain how your agency solves community problems and improves the lives of not only your program's clients but the donor as well. It will be specific. And it will tell your supporters why your nonprofit is worthy of their backing among the alternatives they have.

Your goal is to get your target groups to notice your nonprofit, learn what your agency is doing, and give them opportunities to interact with and spread the word about your organization. And they will—if they can identify with your cause, understand what your agency is about, and see how their goals can best be met by supporting your nonprofit. All the value propositions will be related yet different. You will want to use the language from each constituency group for best results.

Once you have value propositions for each constituency group you want to reach, you can use them for fundraising, outreach, staff recruitment and retention, volunteer recruitment and retention, board member recruitment and retention, and garnering community support. An organizational value proposition can be placed on your website and used for press releases, social media posts, and other general communications. Specific value propositions to get more clients, employees, volunteers, and board members can be used on your individual web pages and in your outreach, recruitment, and retention materials. Value propositions aimed at donors can be included in your case for support and the materials you create from it—for example, brochures, donation pages, annual appeals, corporate giving campaigns, grant narratives, and other fundraising items.

## Make Your PR Count

Nonprofits usually seek visibility by issuing press releases, posting on social media, speaking at events, holding community fundraising activities, and being listed in resource and membership directories. The goal tends to be doing as many of these activities as possible, hoping to raise public awareness of all the good the organization does. After all, the reasoning goes, the more people that hear about the good work we're doing, the more the community will support us. Rarely does it work that way.

Don't get me wrong here. I believe that organizations need to initiate a fair amount of their own publicity. But not in the way nonprofits generally do it, that is, targeting the general public, trying to speak to everyone, talking about the good work their agency does. This approach assumes that a broad audience is interested in your nonprofit and that once they hear about your organization, they will be so bowled over they will support your agency. And those assumptions are not true most of the time.

When you target the whole community, resources are poured into getting a message out to many that only resonates with a few. The return on investment is minimal. To get better results, consider tweaking what you're already doing. Keep issuing press releases, posting on social media, speaking at events, holding community fundraising activities, and being listed in resource and membership directories. Just be more strategic about how you're going about it. Write press releases, social media posts, and speeches that speak to the specific groups you're trying to reach. Have one unique message you repeat again and again. And don't make meeting your nonprofit's goals the center of your promotion. Talk about meeting community goals instead.

Talk to them about meeting their needs and their goals instead of how great your nonprofit is. While you will attract some support for your organization by spouting off its accomplishments, it is not your agency that excites people. It is its mission success. And about how potential supporters can participate in meeting its mission. When you describe mission fulfillment, talk about it as part of its journey to meet its goals. Make it about your agency's mission, not your agency.

For example, which statement has more impact on you. "Last year, my nonprofit fed twelve thousand people," or "last year, you helped twelve thousand hungry people eat healthy meals, reducing the need to steal and helping stave off malnutrition, decreasing the costs to our law enforcement and healthcare systems." Which do you think would garner more donations?

> ### Food for Thought
>
> When you write press releases, social media posts, and speeches, speak to the specific groups you're trying to reach and focus on the community instead of your nonprofit.

Make it about them and their participation in the fulfillment of the mission, not your agency.

## Meet Your Donors' Goals

Most nonprofit external communications involve asking people to give money, attend events, or apply for jobs. Sometimes you also see communications with the purpose of reputation repair and management. A nonprofit organization needs all these to take place to survive. Not so for a community member.

Instead of talking about your agency's goals, survey your different constituencies and find out about their goals. Start with your current volunteers, donors, board members, staff, and advocates. Hopefully, the constituencies you have are the types of people you want to have more of. What drew those already involved in your nonprofit to it? What are their goals for being involved? Why do they stay? Also, survey those who have left and find out why they left. You want to know so that you can build on the positives and correct the negatives. That way, your constituencies will say good things about your organization to other people and spread the word about your agency. They, then, are your ambassadors. And word of mouth is the most effective and least costly way to draw people into your cause.

So, what are donors' motivations to give? What are they hoping to achieve? And how do you, as the lead fundraiser, help them attain their goals?

## Fulfill Individual Donor Motivations

According to the 2016 U.S. Trust Study of High Net Worth Philanthropy, individual donors give for many possible reasons: they believe in the mission of the organization; they believe their gift can make a difference; they experience personal satisfaction, enjoyment, or fulfillment from making the donation; a habit of supporting the same causes annually; they want to give back to the community; and adherence to religious beliefs. According to Network for Good, the number one reason why donors stop giving is that they don't know how their gift is being used. Donors want to positively impact issues they care about and know they made a difference in impacting others.

The implication is that you don't ask for money. You make mission-based asks, the mission being what change can happen in the community as a result of their donation, not the change in your organization or its programs.

And you need to report to your donors how their donations were used. Which means that to tap into their motivations, you don't report on program outcomes. Instead, you report on the changes the donation made in the human condition. It is not the money or the organization that is important to donors. Their goal is to increase mission fulfillment.

So, help them reach that goal. Base your ask on the amount of mission your nonprofit can meet through their donations and report back to them that you did exactly that. It's all about mission.

I would also add that donors want to be acknowledged. It is a human need to be acknowledged and validated. Always treat donors with honor, dignity, and respect, one way to acknowledge their worth as human beings. Acknowledge and thank them for their gifts as well.

> **Warning!**
> Center your fundraising efforts around the needs of your potential donor, not your organization.

Most nonprofits do not thank their donors in a timely fashion, if at all. That's a huge mistake. Your donors need to be honored for their contributions, no matter how small the monetary value. That's how you get people to give again—acknowledge, honor, and appreciate them for what they have chosen to do on your agency's behalf.

Help donors meet their goals. Talk mission, not money. And then show them they accomplished what they set out to do.

## Meet Foundation Objectives

Foundations' goals are to meet the legal objectives under which they were formed. If they do not meet their legal objectives, they are going to have legal problems. They give money away according to their stated missions.

Foundations are nonprofits, too. They must abide by the charitable purposes for which they were established. Foundations do not give money away to fulfill your nonprofit's mission. Foundations give away money to fulfill *their* missions. Your chances of funding are greater if you do your research first and match your organization's mission to theirs. In other words, you help them meet their goals.

And you need to follow their guidelines. Don't try to fit a square peg into a round hole. They have guidelines for a reason. Their guidelines help them meet their objectives in some way, whether we understand them or not. Always follow the guidelines they give. Help them meet their goals.

You also need to complete and submit your reports on time. Foundations need to report on how well they achieve their objectives. They need to know how much of their mission your agency was able to meet. Accurate and thorough reporting is essential. It helps the foundation justify the money it gave to your organization. It is through the reports that they know if they met their goals.

## Help Businesses Make Money

Businesses know it is good for them to give back to their communities. Communities are where companies sell their products or services, hire their employees, and make their impact. Most businesses want to be good corporate citizens. Help them do that. Partner with them to fulfill your organization's mission. Report back on their donation's impact—to both them and the community.

But remember, companies are in business to make money—not give it away. So, when you approach businesses, don't only ask for money to meet your mission; ask to enter into a mutually beneficial partnership that helps you meet their mission *and* money goals.

So, what are their money-making goals? How do businesses make money? By:

- Increasing visibility of their products or services among their target markets;

- Acquiring new customers;

- Increasing existing customers' loyalty; and

- Reducing their operating costs.

If your nonprofit can help companies meet any of their goals, you may be well-positioned to get a big donation.

The key to giving them visibility is not just promoting them; it's promoting them to their specific target market, that is, to people who are most likely to buy their product or service. The trick is knowing who their target markets are and seeing if your nonprofit interacts or communicates with those specific audiences. One of your audiences, for example, your clients, staff, volunteers, or donor base—may be one of their target markets. How can you design opportunities where you can benefit from a donation and they can benefit by exposure to their target markets? It can be ethically done.

You can also boost your business case for support by talking their language. For example, can you intelligently talk about your nonprofit's market demand and penetration? Do you have numbers to back up your claims? Do you talk about your brand and unique market position? Do you talk about how your brand can increase *their* brand, thus increasing customer and employee loyalty, thereby reducing marketing, recruitment, and retention costs? If you can speak their language and address their concerns, you have a strong case for support. Because you're addressing *their* money concerns as well as your mission ones. It's called cause marketing, where companies engage in philanthropic relationships for the dual purposes of doing good and increasing profits. And it is a powerful fundraising tool. Use it to your advantage.

## Be Consistent in Your Messaging

To reach specific groups with your nonprofit's message, you need to tell them precisely what you do and how you do it. You need to communicate the values that permeate your organization. You must determine the words, phrases, and symbols that best speak to the world the essence of your nonprofit.

Each constituency will value something slightly different about your nonprofit. You may tailor the message's delivery and the value propositions you relay to each group, but your core message should remain the same. That way, your message is always based on their goals and perceptions, instead of just yours. And there is no doubt about who your nonprofit is and what it stands for. That identity is what you want to be repeated in the community again and again.

### Food for Thought

To rise above the noise and be noticed in the fray, work on creating a consistent brand, articulating a unique marketing position, getting everyone in your organization to iterate one message, and repeating your message extensively among your target groups.

## Articulate a Unique Marketing Position

A unique marketing position defines what a company brings to the market that is unique, that is, what sets it apart from all other companies like them. Your nonprofit's unique-marketing-position statement tells the world where your agency fits into the landscape of all the other nonprofits, what your nonprofit's niche is, and what makes your organization different than others like yours. Knowing your unique marketing position is paramount. To be competitive in the resource acquisition game, you need to tout your nonprofit's uniqueness just as much as for-profits do.

You formulate your unique marketing position statement by taking your agency's perceptions of itself, your clients' perceptions of your agency, your donors' perceptions, your competitor's perceptions, and the community's perceptions and figuring out the one thing all those perceptions have in common. In that one thing they have in common lies your unique value to the market. Once you know how you are different than everyone else, then you can start building clear, unifying messages around it.

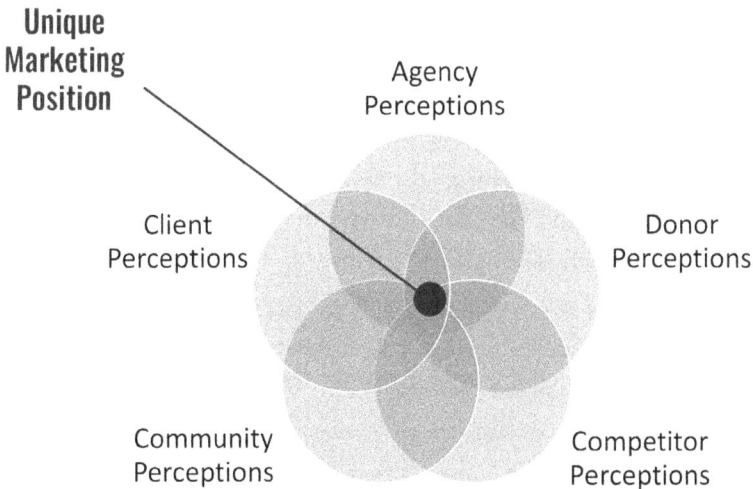

**Unique
Marketing
Position**

Agency
Perceptions

Client
Perceptions

Donor
Perceptions

Community
Perceptions

Competitor
Perceptions

What does your nonprofit do that no other nonprofit does? You may be able to think of characteristics to describe your agency, but your words may not accurately reflect the voices of your different constituencies. Survey your various constituencies to see how they describe your organization. Ask them what they find most exciting about your nonprofit. Ask them why they choose to be involved with your agency. Do your homework. Get the facts. Know for certain how your nonprofit is perceived in the community.

## Create a Consistent Brand

Your nonprofit's brand, roughly speaking, is its reputation for how well it lives up to its promises. A strong brand means your nonprofit is widely known to make a positive impact on the issues it tackles. In other words, your agency demonstrates a strong commitment to its mission.

Building your brand starts with communicating it. And your nonprofit's brand is conveyed through every symbol, word, and action associated with the organization. That includes internal and external communications and materials. You want your internal people all to be on the same page to impart the same distinctive message to the public. And you want to share a singular, powerful message to your external audiences so they know exactly who your nonprofit is and there is no confusion over what it stands for. That means your logo, font, website, photography, public speeches, social media posts, brochures, reports, volunteer trainings, employee manuals—everything you do and say—is planned, coordinated, and embedded with the same language, concepts, and symbols.

It also means choosing and designing fundraising activities that promote the message you are trying to communicate. All these components combined make a strong brand.

Your organization's brand is unique to it. Therefore, think about the kinds of activities that will support *your* nonprofit's mission and convey *your* agency's messages. Don't just copy someone else. Build *your* brand. Strengthen your reputation in the community. You will be better off for it in the long term. Because strong brands are attractive to potential supporters. And community support is what you're looking for.

Your agency's logo may be the most familiar symbol of your essence. And you may think that you develop a logo based on what the decision-makers like and dislike. Not true. In fact, branding is big business in the for-profit world and can cost hundreds of thousands of dollars. And it is based on careful research and objective data.

To create a logo that communicates the essence of an organization, a branding firm will ask a sample of your nonprofit's internal and external constituencies to contact for feedback. Branding professionals know the questions to ask to get the best responses. And they have knowledge that we don't. For example, they know that color evokes an emotional response. And that the colors that you use are an important part of how people experience your organization. For a quick and dirty look, Google your logo's color meanings and see what emotions are elicited when people see your agency's logo.

Same with fonts and pictures. What fonts you use communicate aspects of your agency's personality. As do the type of pictures and photos you use in your communication materials. Every aspect of your communication materials tells people something about your organization. A branding firm can help you identify all those aspects. The goal is to develop one unified image of your nonprofit that you can use to tell the world about you. So that everyone in the community who comes across you gets the same message, in both word and image.

If you have the connections and can get a branding firm to do some pro bono work on your behalf, great. You may also be able to garner a capacity-building grant that will cover the project expenses. If you can't get something donated or funded, shop around and find a consultant you can afford. The money is worth the investment. The long-term benefits of good branding leading to more community support far outweigh the short-term financial costs.

## Make Your Message a Mainstay of Your Culture

That means training all your core constituencies to repeat the same message. Which means your unique messaging needs to be incorporated into your organizational culture. Which means it is in your board recruitment materials, board agenda, promotional materials, speeches, press releases, fundraising campaigns, events, staff training manuals, volunteer training materials, and any other tool you use to communicate about your nonprofit, internally and externally. Your goal is to provide your bullseye groups with the messages they need to spread the word out to the next circle. And then the circle after that. It's a ripple effect. Community awareness of your nonprofit increases as each circle expands. And, since you are coming from their perspectives using their words based on their values, potential community supporters will understand what you're trying to say. Which, in turn, results in a greater likelihood they will respond.

You want to make sure you drill the message down to the staff and volunteers inside the organization, too. The biggest and least expensive communication channel for getting your message out to the community is your paid and unpaid staff. Employees spend most of their waking hours at work. Volunteers know your agency from personal experience. They talk to their families, friends, neighbors, and colleagues. Who speak to their spouses, friends, neighbors, and colleagues.

So, make sure your messaging is consistent in your strategic plan, marketing plan, communications plan, and case for support. Especially since these documents lay the basis for your external communications. Also, make sure the language you use to describe your nonprofits is included in your staff and volunteer training manuals.

## Spread Your Message Extensively

The key to getting your message noticed by the community is that it is easy to understand and heard often. Put your agency's message everywhere, in every communication vehicle you use. For example, the logo on your letterhead; the look, feel, and content on your website; in your social media posts; in your newsletter articles; in your press releases; during radio and TV interviews; in your public speeches; in your fundraising appeals, including grants, annual appeals, and major gift and capital campaign materials; and in your promotional materials, to name a few.

Again and again, spread the same core message in every piece of information your nonprofit produces, modified for different target audiences. Gaining visibility among a specific target group. Going where they are. Searching them out. Using the least amount of resources for the most amount of gain. And, with the extremely limited amount of resources most nonprofits operate with, using those resources to get as much value as you can. Yes. You can do it.

## Invite People In

It's not enough to be visible to potential supporters. You have to ask them to join you in your cause. And you have to ask them directly, clearly, and specifically. You want to leave no question as to what you want them to do. No, you're not being pushy. You're being forthright and honest. People appreciate that.

That means always have some sort of call to action in your communications. Tell people how they can best help you. Give them direction. Be the leader and ask them to follow. Donate now. Visit your state representative. Register here. Save my seat. Tell me your opinion. Volunteer. Vote. Whatever you're doing, make it clear how you want other people to join you.

And make it easy for them to do so. How easy is it for people to get involved with your organization? What are the obstacles? How can you remove them? Do your processes work for everyone in your target group, including people who are different than you? Is your language offensive in any way? Are your images diverse? Make getting involved with you as easy and inviting as you can.

Which means you need periodic feedback from people regarding their experience with you. You won't know unless you ask. Don't just assume you know. Even if the results are what you expected, you have objective evidence that what you say is true after the survey. That the community thinks what you think. That you really are inviting and easy to deal with. Which can help you attract more potential supporters. Which is what your goal is.

## Ask Them to Get Involved

Every public message you deliver—be it a press release, social media post, advertisement, or speech, to name a few—should have a call to action with a clear way to get involved in your organization's work. Whether you ask them to like and follow you on social media to help you spread the word, advocate for policy change that will improve the world they live in, vote so their voice is heard, come to an event to meet like-minded people, or donate to further the cause they believe in—whatever it is—you must ask. If you don't ask, you don't get. Always have a clear call to action.

**Words of Wisdom**

Ask, and you shall receive

And in your call to action, tell them the benefit to them of completing whatever you're asking them to do. Notice how I added a 'why it's important' phrase when I listed some things you could ask people to do. It's important to outline the benefits of completing what you've asked them. Let them know how they will fulfill their values and reach their goals by performing that task. Understand their motivations. Use the information you found when surveying them. Again, make it about them, not your nonprofit or its needs.

## Provide Meaningful Experiences

And then just don't put them to work doing anything. Design ways for them to get involved around their needs, not yours. What are they interested in doing? What do they find meaningful? Take the time to find out so they feel fulfilled in their work and become enthralled with your organization. Yes, you need some structure. No, it can't be completely individualized. But you *can*, and want to, customize for groups of people.

Which is why you survey your different constituencies. To find out what they as a group find motivating. Because then you can design opportunities that fit a majority of the group's needs and find efficiencies in your operations while garnering the kind of goodwill you need to attract more volunteers, donors, good board members, motivated staff, and community advocates. Fulfill them. Help them achieve the satisfaction they crave. And they will love your organization, stay with your nonprofit, and spread good things about your agency to others. And others will eagerly want to be involved.

## Convert Supporters to Donors

Sooner or later, you want those community supporters to convert to donors. After your initial approach, it's time to build relationships that culminate in an ask for money.

Start by validating the people you interact with. That doesn't mean you necessarily agree with them. It means you listen to them until they feel heard and understood. Acknowledge their values, beliefs, likes, and preferences. Accept who they are in their entirety. People yearn to be acknowledged and accepted. You can meet that need.

Approach them with an attitude of gratitude. Thank them for their time and interest. Thank them at the beginning of the interaction and again at the end. They have chosen to spend a portion of their life responding to you. Be honored. Stay positive. Be a bright spot in their day. People tend to respond to others in the same way they are approached. Expect the best. Assume the noblest. Always give a potential donor the benefit of the doubt. Do your best to make that person feel that they have helped you have a better day.

Take one step at a time. One *baby* step at a time. Talk about the process of developing a relationship. Ask about the next steps. Then follow up on your conversation. Especially if you reached an agreement on what would happen next. Relationships need continued time and attention. Give them.

## Getting the Most out of Exciting Your Community

I know it's counterintuitive, but you will improve your visibility in the community by targeting the groups you want to reach. And that means offering fundraising opportunities that appeal to particular donor groups. For example, a younger donor will probably respond more readily to a peer-to-peer text campaign than a direct mail appeal. If you want to acquire younger donors, a direct mail appeal is probably not your best choice. It's all about your target groups' needs, values, and preferences.

Relay unified, consistent messages to your community to mobilize it to support your nonprofit's mission. You will need to empower your board to carry that message, as we talked about in **Chapter Six** and mobilize your staff to be your ambassadors, as we discussed in **Chapter Seven**. Start by attracting supporters of all kinds. Invite them in and make it easy and rewarding for them to participate. And then ask them for financial support. Don't ask them for money, though. Don't make it a transaction. Transactions are one and done. Make it *transformational*. Make it about them changing the world through the support of your nonprofit. It's not about what your agency does. It's about what they do. Then financial support will grow.

## How It Worked in Real Life

"That's great," you say. "But I've tried and tried and haven't been able to penetrate my community to the extent I want." Well, let me tell you how we did within the four nonprofits we are following in this book.

### Regional First Responder Assistance Agency

Since this organization wanted to generate more donations from younger donors, the first thing we did to excite the community about its mission was to identify the target group it wanted to reach, in this case, people who were in their thirties and forties, as opposed to the people in their fifties who comprised most of its board and sixties and older who comprised most of its donor base. We did some research and learned how the different age cohorts were different from one another. We looked at the different generational histories, needs, values, goals, and communication preferences. Then we designed a communications outreach program that the younger cohort would be more likely to respond to.

Then together we worked on messaging. We created a case for support that reflected the needs, values, and goals of the cohort we were trying to reach. We revised their fundraising materials to be consistent with the case for support and its messaging, including their annual campaign, major gift materials, and website content. Because this agency had already reached out to local businesses, met some of the needs of its business community, and developed solid relationships with them, we also created materials that local businesses could share with their customers and employees.

We also worked on PR and communications. Luckily, the agency was in the process of hiring a part-time social media specialist who was tech-savvy and identified with the younger age group. The executive director shared the support case and directed her to have messaging consistent with it. And, since one of its strengths was its volunteer structure and development, we highlighted the meaningful involvement people could make to the organization, financially and otherwise.

Because this nonprofit had deep relationships with the community, it asked its contacts to help spread the word about the agency. Since the support case highlighted the benefits to the community, they shared the case for support, which was received well. Their existing business and volunteer contacts agreed to do what they could do for the organization. So, area businesses posted flyers in their windows, volunteers put signs on their lawns, and the local press featured them multiple times. Since they had unified messaging, all constituencies got a clear sense of who the organization was, what it stood for, and the benefits of engaging with it.

It wasn't long before the organization started attracting the business and younger donors it craved.

## Statewide Domestic Violence Transitional Housing Agency

Since this was a large agency with many different departments, the first thing we did here to excite the community about their mission was to understand how the departments worked together. Then we created messaging that all agreed served their purposes. We developed easily implementable techniques to infuse their department's staff with the messages we wanted them to communicate to the public. To motivate them to share our messages, we worked on getting the messages through agency communication channels to highlight staff contributions to important community initiatives and agency fundraising efforts.

In addition, we worked on coordinating agency communications. The agency newsletters, press releases, and fundraising were all overseen by the development director. That way, the messages in the communications vehicles would be consistent with the grants, event speeches, and business meetings. The agency could then present one unified front to all its community constituencies.

Because this agency wanted to pursue corporate support, we created an introductory business packet highlighting the financial and mission strength of the organization, as well as opportunities for mutually beneficial involvement. We also started a business networking group with regular meetings. The meeting agendas reflected the messaging we had created. So that businesses could see how the agency could benefit them and the community, we included agency client and business relationship testimonials on the agenda.

It wasn't long before this agency had a strong community business support network—a constituency outside its previous circle of support.

## Community Drug Prevention Agency

This agency was most in need of reputation repair. Important donors had started questioning the viability of the organization.

The first thing that we did here was to create a letter sent to all major donors explaining where the agency was in its growth cycle and what was being done to address the issues.

Next, we worked on strengthening the organization's communication channels. We developed a quarterly email newsletter for volunteers and donors, attaching opportunities for financial sponsorship outlining the PR opportunities available to the sponsor. We worked on list building to broaden our distribution.

During our time together, the agency also had a wonderful opportunity for pro bono professional branding services. We identified our key constituencies, the branding agency conducted field research, and developed a complete brand package, including a messaging playbook. The playbook was invaluable. They used the messaging in their press releases, newsletters, grant proposals, and annual appeals. They also used it to revise their board recruitment materials, volunteer outreach efforts, board and volunteer training manuals, and employee handbook. We were determined to infuse the messaging into the organizational culture.

The nonprofit soon started reaping the benefits of its efforts. Financial support increased. More people wanted to volunteer. It became known in the community as a small but mighty organization moving forward. It had begun redefining itself, and it was working.

## International Maternal Health Education Agency

Still early in its life cycle, this nonprofit was well known within its circle of influence and had no problems expanding its programs. Its immediate need was to structure a fundraising system that attracted general operating support. And that meant stepping up its communication and fundraising efforts to reach a broader audience.

The first thing to do was survey board and staff leadership, conduct a SWOT analysis, and develop a case for support. This case then informed the development of its board and staff training materials. We then trained the board and staff in the messages we wanted them to relay to the community. The messages we wanted them to relay focused on its mission in action while keeping client confidentiality.

Since this agency wanted to increase its individual donor base, expand the foundation support, and initiate a corporate giving program, the messaging from the support case informed its appeals, grant writing, and business asks. As it was also beginning its PR efforts, the messaging was also used in its social media outreach and annual report. By integrating its communications and fundraising, its messages to the community were unified and consistent, leading to a larger presence in the community.

We also worked on creating mutually beneficial fundraising asks based on its mission. This was particularly important to the development of the foundation funding and corporate giving programs. Instead of trying to reach just any foundation or business, we identified prospects that had some relation to its mission, operations, board, staff, or client base. I did the initial research and then trained the staff on how to approach these potential supporters.

By the end of the engagement, they were ready to move to the next phase of donor development.

## Bringing It Together

If you want to raise more money, start by fulfilling individuals' motivations for giving, foundations' obligations to their legal objectives, and businesses' goals of giving and making money. Meet your donors where they are. Show them how a relationship with your organization helps them meet their objectives. Raise more money by focusing on your giving partners and their desires. Meet your goals by meeting theirs.

You start by identifying, researching, and then speaking to the specific groups you want to reach. You identify who you want to reach by building on the support of the groups you already have, your bullseye. Do your research and find out all about these groups: their demographic characteristics, likes, dislikes, values, where they hang out, and how they communicate with one another. And then design your outreach to reach them where they are through the communication channels they use in ways they are likely to respond to. And you do this for each group you're trying to reach.

To gain the community support you desire, adapt some of the concepts from the field of marketing. Allocate resources such that your organization will reach people with a propensity toward your cause, not just anybody. You want to expend your resources where they are most likely to bear fruit. Get the most out of your scarce resources.

Spread your message extensively. Repeat it often, both internally and externally. Make sure your message is unified so there is no confusion about who your nonprofit is and what it stands for. You want a strong community image.

It takes time and effort to build potential donor relationships. Time and effort that is precious. Set yourself up for success. Target narrow donor groups. Research and learn about your donors. Get evidence of what they think and use that information to create effective communication campaigns.

Know your supporters inside and out so that you can invite others who have the same values to join you in ways they understand and will respond to. Then ask people to do what you want them to do. Ask directly, clearly, and specifically. Make sure it is easy and inviting for people to interact with you. Regularly ask for feedback on your supporters' experiences.

Approach prospective donors with honor, gratitude, and respect. Acknowledge and validate what is important to them. And you will have laid the groundwork for making the ask for money.

You will excite your community, stand out in the crowd, increase community support for your nonprofit, and gain new donors by executing this plan.

## Points to Remember

- The competition for funds is fierce. To be in the running for the most funds, you must stick to your mission in all you do, including your fundraising. You want to be known for the mission your nonprofit meets instead of being poor or greedy, always asking for money. To get the most and highest donations, meet your donor's needs first.

- Good PR and marketing include more than press releases, social media campaigns, website development, speaking engagements, media coverage, advertising, organizational memberships, resource list inclusion, and hosting community fundraising events. Target your efforts to specific groups you have identified as the most crucial and thoroughly research them to get the best results.

- Create and maintain consistent, strong messaging through good branding, articulating a unique marketing position, making your message a mainstay of your culture, and spreading your message extensively.

- When you approach potential donors, invite them in, ask them to get involved, and provide meaningful experiences in which they can participate.

## What's Next?

Now that I've emphasized the importance of targeting specific groups with consistent messages, what do you do next? How do you begin to know what your donors' likes and preferences are? That's the topic we discuss in the next chapter.

## Chapter Ten

# Donor Tastes

I t's not enough to know what you and your nonprofit need regarding money coming in. You also need to see the donation process from the donor's point of view, that is, know what different kinds of donors give, who they give to, and how they give. Different donor groups give to different causes in different ways. You want to customize your fundraising elements to fit their likes and preferences, so they will respond to your campaigns.

This chapter gives you an overview of how different groups of donors give, their likes and preferences, the general donor experience, and what donors want from that experience. Because major donors will want to meet with them, board members should also understand donor motivations and be aware of donor preferences that may be very different than their own.

## The Charitable Giving Pie

Based on research done by The Giving Institute on philanthropic giving, donations from individuals consistently make up about 80 percent of the charitable pie. About 9 percent of individual contributions are bequests. Foundations make up about 15 percent of total charitable giving. For-profit businesses make up the remaining 5 percent. In determining these percentages, philanthropic giving does not include unearned income, earned income (fees for service), or government funding.

# CHARITABLE GIVING IN THE U.S.

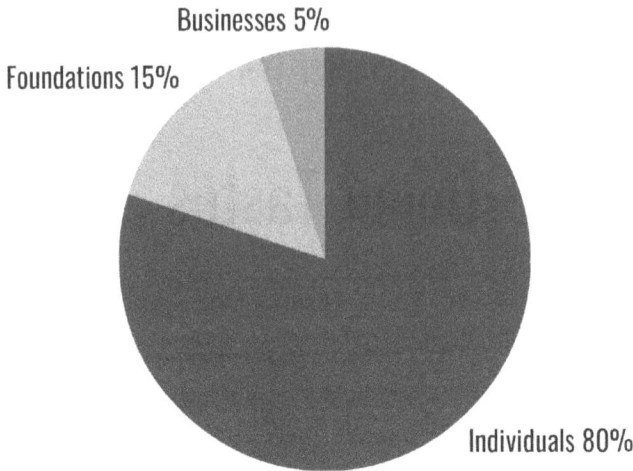

Businesses 5%

Foundations 15%

Individuals 80%

These statistics have implications for what kind of fundraising to pursue. Notice that most of the money comes from individuals, suggesting that nonprofits put their scarce resources there. However, as we learned in **Chapter Five**, average individual gifts hover right around one hundred dollars. The average foundation grant award, by contrast, is twelve thousand dollars. Yet foundations only make up about 15 percent of total giving. The pool of available foundation funding is smaller than that of individuals. Corporate funding makes up even less of total giving, at 5 percent, smaller than both what is available through individuals and foundations.

Even though most donations are realized through individual giving and, as we mentioned in **Chapter Three**, the cost to raise a dollar is least expensive through major gifts, many nonprofits spend most of their fundraising resources pursuing grants and event sponsorships. This is a shame because if resources were redirected, nonprofits would raise so much more. People are lured into overdependence on grants and special events by the big individual awards when, in fact, the biggest percentage of overall giving is through individuals. Perhaps if more nonprofits understood where most of the money lies, they would change their fundraising strategies.

## Why Donors Give

Why do donors give? Different types of donors—individuals, foundations, and businesses—are motivated to give for different reasons.

### Individuals

People are driven by values, feelings, and beliefs. Know donor values, needs, and motivations so you can meet them where they are. Appeal to the underlying values in your asks. Acknowledge the beliefs behind your message.

So, what are the values, feelings, and beliefs around individual giving? Why do people donate? In order of importance:

1. They believe in and have a connection to the mission of the nonprofit.
2. They believe that their gift will make a difference.
3. They experience personal fulfillment through giving.
4. Giving has become habitual.
5. They want to give back to the community.
6. They are fulfilling a religious obligation.

This all means that the best thing you can do to motivate your donors is talk about your agency's mission and how the donor can contribute to making a real difference.

### Foundations

Foundations give to fulfill *their* missions. The question foundations ask is, "Where will our money best be used to achieve our legal objectives?"

Yes, I said legal objectives. Foundations are legally bound to the missions for which they exist. If they do not adhere to their legally stated purpose, they risk losing their tax-exempt status.

### Food for Thought

Whether you pursue individual, foundation, or corporate gifts, the mission is your bottom line. Mission first. Always mission first.

The IRS also requires foundations to give out a certain amount of their corpus every year. That's why the IRS requires foundations to make their tax returns, called 990s, available. So the public knows what they give money to and how they give it out. Researching 990s should be part of every foundation fundraising strategy. Do your research before approaching any foundation. It's public information. Foundations expect you to know it.

## Businesses

Long gone are the days when businesses gave just because you asked. Although there are charitable reasons, smart for-profits meld their philanthropic and strategic business objectives. Today, when you approach and develop relationships with for-profits, you are entering into exchange relationships where both parties give and get something of value. You get the donation, and they get a new avenue to better meet their goals.

So, what are their goals? For-profits are looking to increase market visibility, expand their customer base, increase customer loyalty, and reduce costs. You can meet these goals through your nonprofit's marketing and outreach, improve your agency's brand, and offer employee volunteer opportunities. (We talked about branding in **Chapter Nine**.) Be creative in the use of your communication vehicles to give them visibility. Match the target markets they have with your constituency groups. Point out how your marketing and volunteer opportunities reduce their costs. For more on how to maximize your organization's corporate relationships, see the ***Nonprofit Quick Guide: Best-Kept Secrets to Engaging and Retaining Business Donors.***

## Individual Donor Giving Differences

Giving trends show that different generational cohorts support different fundraising causes, use different gift vehicles, and research nonprofits differently. Using the information about each donor group to customize your fundraising program will drastically increase the response to your appeal and improve your fundraising results. The U.S. Census

Bureau and The Center for Generational Kinetics generational cohort information provide data on generational preferences.

Matures were born in 1945 or earlier. Baby boomers were born between 1946 and 1964. Gen Xers were born from 1965 to 1979. Millennials were born from 1980 to 1995. Generation Z is defined as people born after 1995.

## What People Give To

According to "The Next Generation of American Giving: The Charitable Habits of Generation Z, Y, X, Baby Boomers and Matures" by the Blackbaud Institute, top causes for mature donors include emergency relief, troops and veterans, the arts, advocacy, and election campaigns. Baby boomer donors are top supporters of first responder organizations, human rights, and religious and spiritual causes. Top Gen X donor causes include health services, animal welfare, and environmental protection. Millennials are top supporters of human rights and international development, child development, and victims of crime and abuse.

## How People Give

In the same vein, different generational cohorts respond to different approaches.

Mature donors prefer voice calls and direct mail; however, 30 percent do donate online. They do not respond to text messaging or follow social media.

Forty-nine percent of baby boomer donors give through a monthly giving program. Forty-six percent give through workplace initiatives. Twenty-one percent give through Facebook.

Forty-nine percent of Gen Xers donate through a monthly giving program. Nineteen percent donate through Facebook. They respond to text messaging, email, and social media campaigns. They also respond to phone calls.

Forty percent of millennial donors donate through a monthly giving program. Forty-seven percent give through a website, while 16 percent give through Facebook. They respond best to text messaging and social media, rarely responding to email or voice calls.

Fifteen percent of Generation Z donates to charity, mainly online. Twenty-six percent of Generation Z volunteers.

## How People Seek Information

Likewise, the different generations learn about the nonprofits they are interested in supporting in different ways. Matures tend to rely on printed information, like annual reports and financial statements. Baby boomers glean information from annual reports and websites. Gen Xers like to get their information online and will go to your website and social media to conduct their research. Millennials rely more on their peers and social media. Generation Z goes to social media and social media influencers.

To reach all the donor cohorts, publish an annual report but send it only to your mature donors who want printed information. Send it electronically to your baby boomer donors. Make sure your website is accurate and transparent for the potential baby boomer and Gen Xer donors that will visit it. You may want to include an infographic reporting on your agency's website and links to your audits and 990s. Work hard at establishing a solid social media presence so that potential Gen X, millennial, and Generation Z donors hear about your organization. And ask your millennial and Generation Z supporters to spread the word and share information about your cause and work. In other words, to fundraise effectively, you will need to develop and pay attention to all of your nonprofit's marketing strategies and materials.

# Generational Differences in Giving

| | Matures Born 1945 and earlier | Baby Boomers Born 1946–1964 | Gen Xers Born 1965–1979 | Millennials Born 1980–1995 | Generation Z Born after 1995 |
|---|---|---|---|---|---|
| Top Causes | Religion Local social service Emergency relief Health Children | Local social service Religion Health Emergency relief Children | Health Local social service Animal Children Emergency relief | Religion Children Local social service Health Animals | Children Animals Health Religion Local social service |
| **Ways They Give** | | | | | |
| Mail | 43% | 27% | 14% | 13% | 9% |
| Website | 38% | 35% | 37% | 35% | 38% |
| Social Media | 6% | 11% | 9% | 17% | 21% |
| Text/SMS | 3% | 3% | 8% | 8% | 4% |
| **Preferred Information Sources** | | | | | |
| Google Search | 37% | 46% | 60% | 56% | 37% |
| Social Media | 9% | 9% | 22% | 41% | 48% |
| Organization's Website | 60% | 61% | 64% | 64% | 47% |
| Annual Report | 31% | 29% | 30% | 29% | 18% |
| Financial Statements | 11% | 15% | 11% | 13% | 18% |

## Appealing to Foundations

Before approaching foundations, know who they are. With all the public information out there, particularly their 990s, foundations expect it. And when you approach them, get the details right. When writing your proposals, make sure their names, mailing addresses, and salutations are correct. I see mistakes like this all the time. If the basic contact information is not accurate, if it doesn't mean enough to you to know the most basic facts about them, they may conclude that they should take an equal amount of effort to get to know you and your organization. After all, if you can't get the name or address right, how in the world will you convince them that you can successfully manage a grant, financially or programmatically? The foundation will ask, "How do we know the information we received is trustworthy if you don't pay attention to what you're doing?"

### Food for Thought

Foundations give so that they can fulfill *their* mission. When you do your research and are culling prospects, match your mission to the foundations'.

### Address Financial Capacity

To be a top contender, you, the potential grantee, must have the financial capacity to carry out the grant, particularly for large amounts. What do your attachments say about your financial capacity? Is the request in line with the size of your budget? Does your nonprofit have a clean audit? What does the 990 say about your agency's income trends? What will happen financially to your nonprofit without our gift? Is your organization desperate for funding? What will happen when the foundation gift ends? Will you be able to sustain your efforts? What is your financial position? How much do you have in reserves? What is your debt ratio? Is your organization financially stable? If not, what steps has your nonprofit taken to get there?

You also must outline how foundation money will be used as stated in your request. What proof does your proposal offer to ensure the money will be used the way it is intended? How do they know, particularly if you are financially shaky, that you will be able to deliver on the outcomes you promise? They also will assess the risk of fraud, particularly by studying the description of your financial management practices.

Foundations have legal obligations to use the money as stated in their tax exemption documents. How easy will it be to work with you in conducting their due diligence? Will you provide financial reports on time? What is your agency's staff capacity for meeting the financial reporting requirements? What does the proposal say about your ability to carry out the foundation's administrative requirements? You must tell them.

## Budget Effectively

Foundations evaluate your program budget in light of what you promise in your narrative. Does your budget adequately support your program activities? Are you understaffed, and will you have trouble meeting your stated objectives? Are you overstaffed and don't really need their money? The job descriptions and organizational chart you provide give them their answers.

Are you paying enough to attract and retain qualified workers? Are your staff adequately trained? Are they adequately supervised? What personnel policies and procedures do you have in place to assure quality delivery of services? How do you know they're working? Do you have objective data or outside certifications that your nonprofit is as good as you say it is? Objective data speaks volumes.

Foundations also want to know that what you say you will do is possible during the life of a grant within the amount of the overall funding you are seeking. How big are your goals and objectives? What is your timeline of activities? Is it feasible? Are you overreaching or underreaching? How do you know if you can do what you promise? Your organizational and program history tells them what they need to know.

## Delineate Mission Capacity

A foundation also assesses your nonprofit's capacity to meet your mission through your proposal. What impact will their donation make? Will their gift magnify what you are already accomplishing? How do they know? What proof do you have? The testimonials of the people you serve will help them form an opinion. Your agency's name mentioned in planning and research documents gives you credibility as to your effectiveness. The awards and certifications you've received relevant to your funding request tell them about your credibility in the field. Community survey data help them understand how important you are to the public. To be one of the top contenders, you must include references to your nonprofit's role in the community and how your organization is perceived. To really stand out, you need to tell them how your agency differs from all the others they're reading about.

For more detail on writing successful grants, see the ***Nonprofit Quick Guide: How to Answer the Eight Questions Every Grant Review Committee Asks***.

## Approaching Businesses

You can expose your nonprofit to your business community by curating content on your website to contain keywords that business professionals use in internet searches. You can become involved with your local, regional, and state Chambers of Commerce, Business and Industry chapter, Rotary Club, and other business groups. You can also advertise in business publications; be a guest on business-focused radio and TV programs; contribute articles to business-directed magazines, newspapers, and other publications; or sponsor a business event.

When you meet with executives, dress in business attire. Speak to them using their language. For example, use the word "profit" instead of "net income." When you talk about how much need your nonprofit meets, put it in terms of market penetration. Instead of presenting a case for support, call it a value proposition. Talk about target markets, branding, and market visibility. Show them that you understand them.

If you leave printed materials, make sure they are brief and attention-getting. Use diagrams, graphs, or infographics. A picture is worth a thousand words. Avoid too much text. And make sure what you leave in is relevant to them and their concerns.

Asking for donations from businesses is not just about meeting your needs; it's about meeting their needs too. For more detail about attracting business support, see the ***Nonprofit Quick Guide: Best-Kept Secrets to Engaging and Retaining Business Donors***.

## Where to Start

If you're wondering where to begin acquiring donors, start with your nonprofit's existing relationships, research them, and customize your campaigns to their preferences. Look at board members, staff, donors, volunteers, advocates, and vendors who are already invested in and familiar with your agency. Then ask them to reach out to their connections. Start with the bullseye and work

### Food for Thought

When you look for donors, start with your inner bullseye, those individuals and entities with whom you have existing relationships, and work outward.

your way out. Then recruit potential donors who don't have any relation to your agency but are interested in your cause. We explored how you can recruit supporters with whom you have no existing relationship in **Chapter Nine**.

## The Donor Experience

Donors will give and give again based on how satisfactory the donor experience is to them. A donor experience the series of interactions a person takes from first becoming aware of your nonprofit to the point of donating, your brand touchpoints, and the physical environment involved in giving to your agency.

The donor journey starts with donors experiencing dissatisfaction with the status quo. They want change to the current human condition. So they start looking for solutions for implementing the change they want to see. At this stage, they may or may not become aware of your nonprofit. If your nonprofit is visible to them and they like what they see, they may decide to interact with your organization. If the interaction occurs, they will evaluate their experience with your agency.

If they are satisfied with the interaction, they may choose to interact again. If they are dissatisfied with the interaction, they may choose to complain about it with you, someone else within your agency, or someone outside your agency. Or they may decide to end the relationship.

The act of complaining constitutes another interaction, which is of itself evaluated. As repeated interactions occur, the donor forms an opinion about your organization, which they may or may not share with you, someone else within your agency, or someone outside your agency.

If interactions continue, sooner or later you will ask for a donation. And if the donor is satisfied with the sum total of all the interactions and has the means to do so, they may make a donation. Mapped out, it looks something like this:

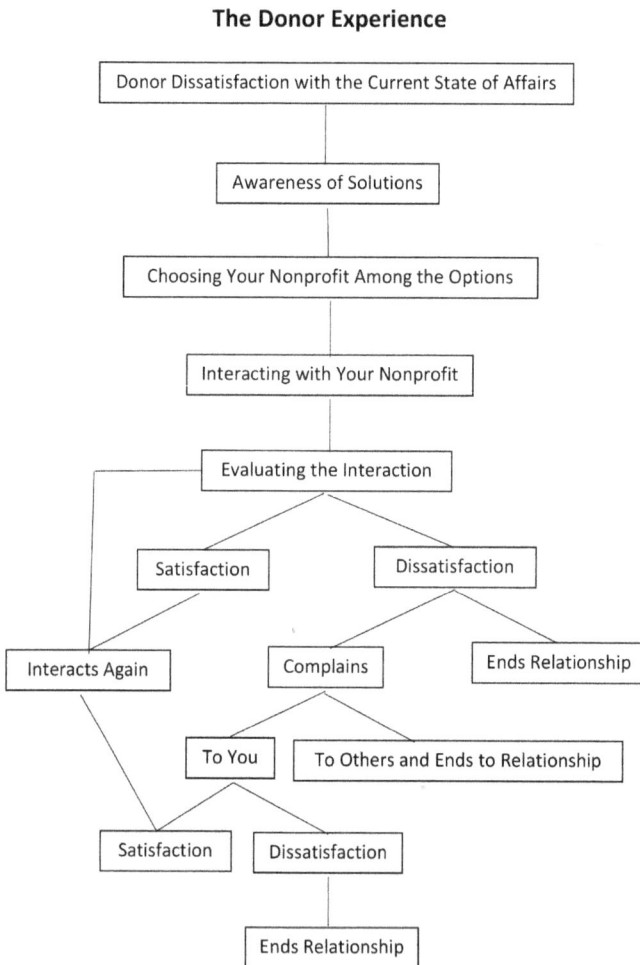

**The Donor Experience**

```
        Donor Dissatisfaction with the Current State of Affairs

                        Awareness of Solutions

                Choosing Your Nonprofit Among the Options

                    Interacting with Your Nonprofit

                      Evaluating the Interaction

              Satisfaction              Dissatisfaction

        Interacts Again        Complains        Ends Relationship

                    To You      To Others and Ends to Relationship

            Satisfaction    Dissatisfaction

                        Ends Relationship
```

As you can see, there are many points where dissatisfaction can occur, and the donor potentially ends their relationship with your agency. Your job is to make the process as smooth and easy as possible so that the vast majority of your donors are satisfied with their experiences when dealing with your nonprofit.

## It's All About Impact

Individual donors are looking to impact an issue, not fix a budget. They are much more interested in hearing about your agency's impact on people's lives than how much money you need. As we pointed out in **Chapter Eight**, the ultimate goal of fundraising is not to how many dollars you want to get. Rather, it is to create a relationship with someone motivated by your nonprofit's mission and show them how they can participate in fulfilling that mission through a financial donation. Successful fundraising strategies focus on how donors can participate in fulfilling the organization's mission within a satisfying relationship.

## Measuring the Donor Experience

The first thing to do is to map out your donor journey. Write down all the possible points of entry into the donation process. For example, potential donors can be volunteers, employees, board members, advocates, community collaborators, business professionals, neighbors, friends, relatives, or clients, among others. Map out all stages of the donation process from beginning to end. Start with how people find you. Include how you reach out to them. Assess the ease of responding to you. Do you have a call to action, that is, a message inviting them to interact with you? What is the process your donor undertakes to respond to your request? Can you or the appropriate person be easily reached? How? Through what channels? Do you have a backup plan if one channel becomes blocked, say, your website crashes or your phones go down? What are other barriers to a satisfactory interaction? How do you know? Have you checked? Do you present a call to action to proceed to the next step? How user-friendly is that process?

Ask the same questions for each step in the journey. And when you have the journey mapped out, test the process to make sure actual results are what you expected and that the process is consistent across various users and user conditions. Test and validate your assumptions.

Then track the number of potential donors who go through each step and calculate your conversion rates. As we mentioned in **Chapter Five**, this is most easily done through constituent relationship management (CRM) software. Some donor management software systems have CRM components, and some have donation tracking abilities. Just make sure that any software you buy has the capabilities to serve your nonprofit's unique needs.

## Improving the Donor Experience

You want the donor experience to be as satisfying as possible so the donor will continue interacting with your nonprofit and give—and give again. Feel-good, memorable experiences don't happen through the act of writing a check. They happen in the context of satisfying relationships. This means that you need ways to engage donors before and after they make their donations. At the very least, thank them. And when you thank them, thank them immediately. And then have a call to action, that is, ask them to do something else. And when they do the next thing, report on the results of their actions. Let them know the impact they made–for the people you serve, not your organization. Remember, always focus on the mission as opposed to money. You want to keep the donor journey going, hopefully resulting in another or a bigger donation. Keep the cycle of thanking, making a call to action, reporting results, and thanking again going.

## Volunteers

One specific type of donation is volunteerism. Although it is not a monetary contribution, volunteering does have an economic value. Volunteers also show great community

**Food for Thought**

According to Volunteer Hub, volunteers are 66 percent more likely to give monetarily to the organizations they volunteer for than those who do not volunteer.

support for your mission in your promotional materials and grant applications. Volunteers can also be prospective donors. Research shows that volunteers are more likely to make financial donations than non-volunteers.

## Characteristics

The Corporation for National and Community Services reports that 25 percent of Americans ages 16 and older volunteer. According to the Bureau of Labor Statistics, people 34-44 years of age, at 29 percent, are the most likely to volunteer. They are followed by people ages 45-54 years at 28 percent; ages 55-64 at 25 percent and 65 and older at 23 percent. Young people ages 6-24 years are the least likely to volunteer, though 24 percent do. Of young people who volunteer, 26 percent of teens volunteer, while only 16 percent of young people ages 20-24 years do.

Volunteers come from all ethnic groups. According to the Bureau of Labor Statistics, of people of Caucasian descent, 26 percent volunteer. This is followed by African descent at 19 percent, Asian descent at 18 percent, and Hispanic/Latino descent at 16 percent.

Volunteers also tend to be more educated than the general population. According to the Bureau of Labor Statistics, 16 percent of volunteers ages 25 years and older have graduated from high school; 27 percent have some college or an associate's degree, and 39 percent hold a bachelor's degree or higher.

According to Volunteer Hub, volunteers spend an average of fifty hours per year donating their time. Half donate fewer than fifty-two hours a year, half more than fifty-two hours. More than 71 percent of volunteers work with only one organization per year. According to the Bureau of Labor Statistics, volunteers work for all types of organizations: 33 percent for religious or spiritual causes; 25 percent at educational or youth-serving nonprofits; 15 percent at social or community nonprofits; 7 percent at hospitals; 5 percent at civic, professional, political, or international organizations; 4 percent at sports, cultural, or arts organizations; 3 percent at environmental or animal causes; and 1 percent at public safety organizations.

Eleven percent of volunteers spend their time preparing or serving food. This is followed by tutoring or teaching at 9 percent; fundraising or selling items at 9 percent; doing general labor or providing transportation at 9 percent; giving professional or management assistance, including serving on a board, at 7 percent; mentoring youth at 7 percent; coaching, refereeing, or supervising a sports team at 6 percent; doing general office tasks at 4 percent; ushering, greeting, or ministering at 4 percent; collecting, making, or distributing clothing, crafts, or other goods at 4 percent; or counseling, providing medical care, or fire/EMT and other protective services at 3 percent. Volunteers engaging in other activities is at 15 percent. Eight percent of volunteers spread their time equally among all causes.

According to the Corporation for National and Community Service, 42 percent of volunteers become involved because they are asked by someone on the organization for which they volunteer; 24 percent are asked by someone in a school; 15 percent are asked by a friend, family member, or co-worker; 2 percent by a boss or employer; and 1 percent by someone else. Thirteen percent came to the organization through some other vehicle.

## Value

All that volunteering time has value. According to Independent Sector, volunteers are worth an average of $28.54 per hour at the time of publication. In addition, they are likely to donate money. According to Volunteer Hub, volunteers are 66 percent more likely to give monetarily to the organizations they volunteer for than those who do not volunteer.

## Bringing It Together

Most charitable dollars are received from individuals, yet many nonprofits pursue grants and special events over large personal gifts. They may realize more net income if they invest more in reaching out to individuals. To appeal to individual donors, understand why they give, how they give, and where they get their information. Foundations don't give because of your nonprofit's mission—they give because of theirs. To appeal to them, research them and get the details right. When writing your proposals, address financial capacity, budget effectively, and delineate mission capacity. Smart for-profits meld their philanthropic and strategic business objectives. To appeal to businesses, come to an agreement about contributions with mutual benefits. Help companies increase their visibility, acquire customers, keep customers, and reduce costs.

To acquire new donors, start with your agency's inner circle and move outward from there. The inner circle consists of your board members, staff, volunteers, advocates, and vendors. Make interacting with you and your agency a good experience. Remember that individual donors are looking to impact an issue, not fix a budget. When they want to get involved, respond to them by inviting them to do something, measuring the quality of their experience, and improving on the experience as needed. And utilize volunteers. Although there is a monetary value associated with their work, the true value is incalculable.

## Points to Remember

Approximately 80 percent of charitable giving is from individuals, 15 percent from foundations, and 5 percent from businesses. Calculations for philanthropic giving do not include earned income, unearned income, or government funding.

- The top two reasons individuals give are they believe in the nonprofit's mission and that their gift will make a difference. Use this information to motivate your donors to give and give again.

- Foundations give to fulfill their missions—not yours. They want to see that your agency has the capacity to carry out the mission plan you described in your proposal.

- The most important tenet to remember when you approach businesses is that you are entering into an exchange relationship where both parties give and receive something of value.

- So that potential and existing donors continue interacting with your nonprofit and giving to it, provide a satisfying experience for them. Feel-good, memorable experiences don't happen through the act of writing a check. They happen in the context of strong relationships.

## What's Next?

So, after implementing all four steps of The Sustainable High ROI Fundraising System, what results did our four nonprofits really realize? Did they, in fact, achieve higher net income, increased organizational capacity, and acquisition of new donors to grow their agencies and advance their missions?

# Chapter Eleven

# A New World Dawns

I t all started with a thorough assessment of their fundraising strengths and gaps. Then we worked concurrently to empower their boards, mobilize their staff, and excite their communities. How have the four nonprofits we've been following fared since they implemented the system? Did the system really work in the long term?

## Regional First Responder Assistance Agency

This nonprofit fared well during and after the engagement. During our engagement, it realized more than an 8 percent increase in individual donations and a 15 percent increase in the number of donors. It also started to acquire the support from younger people it wanted. As of this writing, the positive trends continue.

Board members remain excited about sharing their stories and are more comfortable approaching their connections. They are out of the "you give to mine, I'll give to yours" asking mentality they were in. And they are recruiting and onboarding new board members accordingly.

The staff is working according to the fundraising plan we developed, without being overly taxed. As they started asking for bigger donations, their average gift per donor increased. Their donor retention rate remains high. The organization has a date scheduled for its new donor software system installation.

The organization's volunteer recruitment and training tools, fund-raising materials, outreach instruments, and website have incorporated the new messaging. Its social media specialist has incorporated the messaging into her endeavors, as well. The agency continues to use the communication channels that best reach younger people while maintaining the channels that their older donors like.

The community is responding positively. More people are fundraising for them. Long-term donors are giving higher gifts overall. And more businesses have started to contribute financially.

## Statewide Domestic Violence Transitional Housing Agency

This agency wanted to increase foundation and corporate financial support. It needed greater visibility in the community to do so. Foundation support increased by 100 percent in the first year after the engagement. And businesses responded positively as well. It wasn't long before its corporate donations reached a quarter-million dollars.

The board continues to give at 100 percent. And new interest in fundraising was noticed by the development staff. As previously noted, the board began giving fundraising leads to the staff via the executive director.

Removing the department silos worked wonderfully. Redesigning the communication and reporting systems was a needed improvement. The program, finance, and development staff continue to work together collaboratively. After a while, the program staff got really excited about fundraising. Soon, they started competing with one another to see who could raise the most money.

With consistent messaging in hand and knowing the program and finance staff would support them, the development staff looked into increasing the amount of grant funding they pursued. Foundation research was done. More grants were applied for. More funding was awarded.

The development team also stepped up their efforts to garner corporate funding. With the support of the program and finance departments, fundraising staff continued their business outreach and networking efforts. To make sure they were speaking their target audience's language and meeting their potential business donor needs, the development team revised their corporate outreach materials and mutually beneficial donor packages several times based on the feedback they received during their business networking meetings. It worked. The number of corporate donors increased by 40 percent.

With the added funding, the organization enjoys a strong financial position, grows, and advances its mission.

## Community Drug Prevention Agency

This agency not only survived but is now thriving. Foundation revenue doubled. Individual donations increased by 50 percent. Businesses started contributing. With the increase in revenues, the agency began to rebuild its financial reserves. It was also able to begin an endowment. It now has about six months of operating reserves and an endowment that supports its volunteer recognition programming.

The agency team worked hard to get there. They had to redesign their recordkeeping systems and accountability structures. They also had to create fundraising policies and procedures that governed the influx of new revenue.

Its board is now active in fundraising, not only generating leads for the development director but also initiating fundraising appeals of their own. Knowing how vital its leadership is, 100 percent of board members continue to give. As predicted, potential major donors inquired about board giving. Their gifts were secured, in part, because of the board's giving leadership.

The agency also realized increased foundation funding, in part, because of the level of board support. In addition, foundations felt more comfortable giving to an organization that positioned itself as growing instead of in desperate need of support. Support increased, too, because the staff started including indirect costs in their grant budgets when allowed. In one year, this nonprofit's foundation revenues more than doubled.

Because of the high return on investment, the executive director and board decided to allocate more resources toward developing their individual-giving program. The agency began to run two appeals each year. To increase revenue from their appeals, fundraising staff used the same core message as they did in their grant proposals. As with the foundation requests, it worked. Existing donors gave bigger gifts, and the organization started attracting new donors.

With a new recordkeeping system, the executive director and board knew precisely where they stood financially. The executive director started analyzing events based on total costs. She also infused mission into them. The return on investment was still not high, and today the organization does not hold fundraising events. Instead, they put their energies into annual appeals, major gifts, proposal writing, and community outreach.

They also started asking their volunteers to support the agency financially. The volunteer base has begun to respond as new volunteers are recruited, trained, and onboarded with more of an emphasis on how can do to support the agency, even financially, in moving its mission forward.

This nonprofit went from struggling to flourishing.

## International Maternal Health Education Agency

It was rewarding to work from the ground up with this nonprofit. The board fundraising training was well received. It is a good sign that the board is continuing discussions about fundraising and board giving. They are also growing in number, with several new members interested in how they can help the organization fundraise. All board members recognize the need to garner more unrestricted funding and are aware of the kind of donor inquiries the agency gets when asking for large donations.

The staff has met several of the milestones outlined in the development plan. For example, they have bought, installed, transferred data to, and started using their new donor management software. They have completed several social media appeals. They have also begun reaching out to the foundations and businesses that were identified. And they are actively recruiting their next development staff member.

They use the messaging we developed for their case for support in their grants, appeals, newsletter, annual report, and content on their website. Program staff are using the same messaging as they reach out to their potential leads. A new fundraising culture is beginning to take hold.

It is too early to report on long-term results. However, they are raising general operating support in ways they haven't before. The prognosis for the future is good as long as the organization keeps up its momentum.

## Bringing It Together

As you can see, the same system was applied to each of our four nonprofits, and the system worked. They all wanted to increase revenues by acquiring new donors, be they individuals, foundations, or businesses. To do that, they all needed to reach out and galvanize their community. All of them were served well by unified, consistent messaging their donors and prospective donors could relate to. Each of them saw increased community support for their organizations. To realize efficiencies in the fundraising process and get buy-in from across the organization, they all integrated fundraising with other organizational units, for example, program, finance, or communications. And all of them made changes to their recordkeeping and reporting systems.

What was different was the nonprofits themselves: their missions, geographical scopes, organizational capacities, ages, stages in the life cycle, budgets, financial positions, funding streams, levels of expertise in fundraising, levels of board involvement in fundraising, levels of staff involvement in fundraising, levels of volunteer development and involvement, and community outreach infrastructures. As such, they each needed customized interventions for them to reach their desired outcomes. So, the methods used to apply The Sustainable High ROI Fundraising Systems were customized for each situation.

The results were fundraising programs that were financially more efficient and effective for each nonprofit. These agencies raised more money, expending fewer organizational resources, and realized higher returns on their fundraising investments. The three for which I have long-term results ended up with more financial reserves, money to improve infrastructure, and funds to build long-term financial assets. They all improved their nonprofits' financial positions, allowing them to grow their agencies and advance their missions. Which was why they used the system in the first place.

Applying the strategies outlined in this book will also achieve more net income to grow your agency and advance your mission. By assessing your nonprofit's fundraising strengths and gaps, empowering your board to fundraise, mobilizing your staff to succeed, and exciting your community about your mission, you will build a robust fundraising program that results in more donors and higher donations. You will create an organizational culture that stimulates your board, staff, and community to become consistent mission ambassadors for your nonprofit. You will realize efficiencies that result in raising more money at less cost, increasing your fundraising return on investment.

Be confident that you will raise the money you need for your nonprofit to change the world for the better.

## Points to Remember

- Implementing The Sustainable High ROI Fundraising System can immediately raise more money, acquiring new donors and higher donations. If you keep following the system's strategies, your contributions will increase year after year.

- By applying the techniques described in this book, you will see a greater awareness of your nonprofit in the community, followed by increased financial support.

- Running your numbers, analyzing the metrics, and choosing high-return activities reduce your overall fundraising costs, increasing your net income. Continuing to implement your choices results in ongoing net surpluses.

## What's Next?

In the next and final chapter, I give summaries of what we've covered and provide you with the next steps for moving your agency forward.

# Chapter Twelve

# Moving Forward

nundated. It's where we started in **Chapter One**. You, as an executive director, are inundated with overwhelming responsibilities, fundraising and otherwise. You need a simple way to relieve the pressures of your job so you can take quality time away from the office and not feel like the agency will fall apart.

The Sustainable High ROI Fundraising System will relieve your fundraising angst. Applying the methods outlined in this book, you *will* achieve more net income to grow your agency, advance your mission with less effort, and get more cooperation from your board members than you realize. Not only will you raise more revenues, but you will allocate resources more efficiently, increase organizational capacity, align board and staff fundraising efforts, attract new supporters, reduce your stress, and give you more time to spend with friends and family.

## Assessing Your Fundraising Strengths and Gaps

The first step of the system is to assess your nonprofit's fundraising strengths and gaps. A thorough assessment will evaluate your agency's functions as they relate to fundraising, including governance and management structures, financial performance, marketing and communication efforts, volunteer programs, recordkeeping systems, and technological needs. Then, to achieve resource efficiencies, craft customized fundraising plans to fit your nonprofit's unique profile.

Do a complete and thorough assessment, including board

leadership, fundraising infrastructure and performance, financial health, marketing and communications endeavors, and volunteer recruitment and development as they relate to raising money. Don't leave the assessment to only one person. Even a consultant will work with different people in your organization to get all the information they need. Different people in different roles will have access to needed information and more expertise in one area than others. When you assess, you need a lead person to keep the information and author the reports so that they are in one consistent voice. And regularly assess your situation and progress in meeting your goals. Some areas are best assessed monthly, some quarterly, some annually, and some biannually. Just make sure you regularly evaluate. Especially when there are changes in circumstances.

Many fundraising issues are consistent throughout the nonprofit world, including dedication to mission and need for general operating funds, integrated fundraising systems, community visibility and outreach, and strong messaging. One fundraising plan does not fit all nonprofits, even nonprofits in the same community with similar missions, sizes, or budgets. Because nonprofits come in all shapes and sizes, for best results, create a fundraising intervention customized to your nonprofit's unique characteristics. Your agency's uniqueness must be reflected in your development plans to realize the most from whatever fundraising elements you choose to implement.

Use your assessment results to implement fundraising activities that engage people in your mission and leverage your strengths. And base present plans on present conditions, not past ones. Take the time to regularly evaluate your plans to see if they are still the best option, given your present circumstances. Do what *your* nonprofit, not someone else's, needs to do to raise the most money you can.

## Elements of a Fundraising Program

There are a plethora of ways to raise money. Which activity you choose depends on your skills and your nonprofit's strategic goals and organizational capacity.

Ways people give can include online donations, direct mail, phone-a-thons, text-to-give solicitations, crowdfunding, peer-to-peer campaigns, large personal gifts, donor-advised funds, foundation grants, government contracts, employee matching gifts, sponsorships, special events, capital campaigns, in-kind donations, and volunteer hours. Each method has its own set of pros and cons. Account for them when considering which activities to implement. Also, invest in the most robust technology you can afford that meets your needs.

Invest in donor management software that is easy to use to enter data; compares goals to results; allows you to analyze the performance of single elements as well as by fundraising channel; contains enough space for multiple years of notetaking; has mail merge capabilities that can personalize for name, address, last donation amount, and this year's requested donation amount; can run donor and donation reports including donor history, average gift per donor, donation growth, donor acquisition, and donor retention rates; and tracks who entered what data when. You want to be able to effectively track donations and monitor trends so that you can know what's working and what's not and where to allocate future resources.

## Empowering Your Board

The second step of the system is to empower your board to fundraise. Boards have a duty to be involved in fundraising, but only at the strategic level. Help your board members understand their responsibilities and empower them to fulfill those responsibilities. Instead of burdening them with transactional tasks, ask them to be mission ambassadors for the agency they serve.

Many times, board members don't realize their duty to be involved in fundraising. Board members may also have unrealistic ideas about fundraising and be reluctant to fundraise. And they may confuse board and staff fundraising roles. You can change things. Teach them what they need to know about fundraising and their responsibilities for it.

Boards have a legal obligation to make sure resources are available for mission achievement. Prepare your board to fundraise by properly recruiting them, focusing them on strategy, and engaging them in creating transformations. With proper recruitment, focus on strategy, and engagement in progress, you will see your board get and stay excited about fundraising. You will have board members who understand their roles in fundraising, embrace it, and actively do their part to garner resources to meet the mission they care about.

Develop a board giving policy that allows for participation and sacrificial giving no matter what the income level. One way to do that is to have a board member mandatory-giving policy. Help your board members lead by example. Share board giving inquiries that come from other donors with your board. To overcome their objections to fundraising, don't call it fundraising. Start by breaking down the steps of an ask into specific steps. Don't focus on the money you are trying to raise. Instead, focus on the progress in mission fulfillment they achieved through their actions.

## Mobilizing Your Staff

The third step in the system is to mobilize your staff. Set up your fundraising staff for success. Give them SMART goals to reach. Budget well. Encourage cross-departmental teamwork. And show your staff how they fit into the big picture.

You want your fundraising staff to raise as much money as possible. To do that, focus on your mission. The best fundraisers are organizational ambassadors who talk about their agencies' missions and mission impact. Focus your fundraising on your mission. Fundraising activities that ooze mission, provide funds for the mission, and generate mission support are the ones that will be the most successful, financially and otherwise.

Remember, what gets measured gets done. Set goals that are specific, measurable, action-oriented, realistic, and time-bound (SMART). The SMARTer your goals, the more successful your nonprofit will be in meeting them. Evaluate fundraising performance in relation to them.

Don't set up your nonprofit for fundraising and financial failure. Set up your staff for financial success through your budgeting. Budget realistic revenues and expenses. Budget conservatively, accounting for total costs. Compare returns on investment. Spread your risk by diversifying your revenue streams. Build in a surplus and put a portion of it aside. Avoid the common pitfalls that hinder financial stability and growth. Evaluate total success: financial performance, mission fulfillment, and the strengthening of important relationships.

Paint the big picture, giving your fundraising staff a complete organizational picture. Fundraising staff interact with program, finance, IT, marketing, communications, volunteer training and management, the board, and the community. They work most effectively when they are aware of any internal and external changes to your nonprofit. Help them do their jobs. Build strong teams. Integrate fundraising throughout your nonprofit.

## The Development Team

Staff your development department with fundraising generalists and a grant writer, providing them with adequate administrative and event planning support. To attract and retain good fundraisers, make them part of the team, support them, and pay them fairly. Discuss expectations on both sides.

To be successful, hone your and your development staff's communication, planning, time management, and negotiating skills. They are essential for garnering donations from individual, foundation, corporate, and government donors. Foster your development department's personal and professional growth. Budget for professional development, even if you can only afford to give time. Research shows that the more highly skilled the fundraiser, the more money they can raise. Provide performance incentives for fundraising staff but be ethical about it. Remember, commission-based pay is considered unethical in the field. Instead, establish work processes and conditions that use external motivators and foster the expansion of internal motivators.

Delegate the day-to-day fundraising responsibilities to your development director while keeping your strategic planning, major donor cultivation, culture creation, and board liaison roles. Know that your fundraisers face many obstacles that are out of their control, including community interest in your nonprofit's mission, agency history and capacity, and the overall economy. Work with development professionals who exhibit a passion for your agency's mission, are good relationship builders, utilize a donor-centric customer service approach, and abide by industry standards. To attract good staff, pay them fairly, set realistic expectations, and provide support for them. To keep them, provide external motivators. Give specific praise liberally. Do not pay your fundraisers on a commission basis. Rather, structure the work and work environment such that you foster the development of internal motivators.

You and your development director may clash on issues relating to the face of the agency, how to work with the board, spending on fundraising endeavors, and how to achieve the best financial results. Address conflict with your development director before it begins. Discuss early on both of your wants and expectations for the position. Respect and understand their viewpoint. Treat them as the professionals they are.

If you are the fundraising department, leverage your time and efforts by getting support. Engage your board in fundraising. Mobilize other staff to become mission ambassadors for your organization. And recruit fundraising volunteers from your community.

## Exciting Your Community

The final step of the system is to excite your community. Start by meeting your community's needs to meet your own. Target your efforts on the segments of the community most likely to be motivated by your nonprofit's mission. Know what your agency brings to the market that no other organization like yours does and spread that message. Remember, it is the totality of what your nonprofit looks like, says, and does that communicates your message. When people do respond, provide an inviting experience for them.

The competition for funds is fierce. To get the most and highest donations, meet your donors' needs first. Focus on your giving partners and their desires. Fulfill individuals' motivations for giving, foundations' obligations to their legal objectives, and businesses' goals of giving and making money. Show them how a relationship with your organization helps them meet their objectives.

To gain the community support you desire, adapt some of the concepts from the field of marketing. Allocate resources such that your organization will reach people with a propensity toward your cause, not just anybody. Target narrow donor groups. Research and learn about your donors. Get evidence of what they think and use that information to create effective communication campaigns. You want to expend your resources where they are most likely to bear fruit.

Get the most out of your scarce resources. Start by identifying, researching, and then speaking to the specific groups you want to reach. You identify who you want to reach by building on the support of the groups you already have, your bullseye. Do your research and find out all about these groups: their demographic characteristics, likes, dislikes, values, where they hang out, and how they communicate with one another. And then design your outreach to reach them where they are through the communication channels they use in ways they are likely to respond to. Do this for each group you're trying to reach.

Create and maintain consistent, strong messaging through good branding, articulating a unique marketing position, and making your message a mainstay of your culture. Spread your message extensively. Repeat it often, both internally and externally. Make sure your message is unified so there is no confusion about who your nonprofit is and what it stands for.

You want a strong community image. Know your supporters inside and out so that you can invite others who have the same values to join you in ways they understand and will respond to. Approach prospective donors with honor, gratitude, and respect. Acknowledge and validate what is important to them. Invite them into your agency, ask them to get involved, and provide meaningful experiences for them.

Then ask people to do what you want them to do. Ask directly, clearly, and specifically. Make sure it is easy for people to interact with you. Regularly ask for feedback on your supporters' experiences.

## Next Steps

You are interested in raising money. Your donors aren't, though. Donors are interested in making an impact on an issue they care about. Focus on your nonprofit's mission rather than your need for money to attract more people to your cause. A mission emphasis will always produce the best results regardless of the funding channel, whether individuals, foundations, businesses, or government.

Engage in strategic planning. Good strategic planning keeps the board and staff on the same page. Setting targets and showing your progress in reaching them motivates your board and staff to move forward while showing the community that exciting things are happening at your nonprofit.

And use the system I am sharing with you. As we saw with the four agencies we followed, The Sustainable High ROI Fundraising System enables you to grow your agency's financial reserves, improve infrastructure, and build long-term financial assets that solidify your nonprofit's financial position, allowing your agency to increase its impact and advance its mission. If you assess your organization's fundraising strengths and gaps, empower your board to fundraise, mobilize your staff efficiently, and excite your community about your mission, you will realize more awareness of your nonprofit in the community, increased community support, increasingly larger donations, a more extensive donor base, reduced overall fundraising costs, and ongoing net surpluses.

## For More Information

To learn more about what your nonprofit can do to move ahead, contact me and schedule a complimentary thirty-minute strategy session with me. We will clarify the fundraising issues your nonprofit is facing, explore possible solutions, and develop a plan to move forward. When you make your appointment, you will be asked a few brief questions about your situation so that I am best prepared to help you.

I can be reached through my website at www.joanneoppeltcourses.com.

# Sample Brief
# Board Fundraising Policies

These board policies are general in nature and do not cover the specific details relating to any one organization. To develop complete policies that meet the total needs of your nonprofit, confer with legal counsel.

## Sample Board Giving Policy

The board is responsible for ensuring adequate resources for mission fulfillment. Board leadership is crucial to attaining strong community support. As leaders of the organization, board members are expected to set the example by making at least an annual financial contribution according to their personal means.

## Sample Gift Acceptance Policy

Because [Nonprofit] actively solicits donations to fulfill and grow its mission and because there is the potential for controversy if certain gifts are accepted, the organization has adopted the following gift acceptance policy:

When determining whether to solicit or accept gifts, the organization will consider whether:

- The acceptance of the gift compromises any of the core values of [Nonprofit].

- There is compatibility between the intent of the donor and the organization's use of the gift.

- Acceptance of the gift will damage the reputation of [Nonprofit].
- The primary benefit is to [Nonprofit] versus the donor.
- Accepting the gift is consistent with [Nonprofit]'s prior practice.
- The gift is offered in a form that [Nonprofit] can use without incurring substantial expense or difficulty.
- The gift will encourage or discourage future donations.

All decisions to solicit and/or accept potentially controversial gifts will be made by the board's executive committee in consultation with the executive director. The primary consideration will be the impact of the gift on the furtherance of the mission.

# Essential Fundraising Evaluation Metrics

## Gross Donation Revenue

Gross donation revenue is the total amount of donations recognized over a specific reporting period before deducting the cost to raise the donations. Trends in gross fundraising revenue indicate the ability of your nonprofit to garner donations.

## Fundraising Net Income

Net income is the total amount of donations your nonprofit realized minus fundraising expenses over a specific reporting period. Trends in fundraising net revenue indicate your nonprofit's ability to realize a surplus

## Average Gift Per Donor

The average gift per donor is calculated by dividing the amount of donations received by the total number of donors that gave during the same period.

$$\frac{\text{Total Amount of Donations Received}}{\text{Total Number of Donors}}$$

## Cost to Raise One Dollar

To calculate your costs to raise a dollar, divide your fundraising expenses by your fundraising revenues.

$$\frac{\text{Fundraising Expenses}}{\text{Fundraising Revenues}}$$

## Donor Acquisition Rate

Your donor acquisition rate tells you the rate of growth of your donor base. Your donor acquisition rate is calculated by dividing the difference between the number of donors this year minus the number of donors last year divided by the number of donors last year.

$$\frac{(\text{Number of Donors This Year} - \text{Number of Donors Last Year})}{\text{Number of Donors Last Year}}$$

## Donor Retention Rate

Your donor retention rate tells you the percentage of total donors that made a second gift. Your donor retention rate is calculated by dividing the total number of repeat donors this year by the total number of donors last year.

$$\frac{\text{Number of Repeat Donors This Year}}{\text{Number of Total Donors Last Year}}$$

## Donor Acquisition Cost

To calculate your cost to acquire a donor, divide the expenses used to recruit new donors by the number of new donors.

$$\frac{\text{New-Donor Recruitment Costs}}{\text{Number of Donors This Year}}$$

## Donor Retention Cost

To calculate the costs of retaining a donor, divide recurring fundraising expenses by the number of recurring donors.

$$\frac{\text{Recurring Fundraising Expenses}}{\text{Number of Recurring Donors}}$$

## Return on Investment

Return on investment tells you how well your resources are financially performing. The ratio expresses what percentage of your gross revenues are devoted to costs. To calculate return on investment, divide net income by expenses.

$$\frac{\text{Net Income}}{\text{Expenses}}$$

# Sample Development Staff Job Descriptions

## Development Director

### Job Summary

The development director oversees all agency fundraising initiatives, including managing donor relationships, interacting with donors to encourage giving, and seeking out sponsorships.

### Responsibilities and Duties

- Develop a strong case for support.
- Create the annual development plan.
- Create and monitor budgets to ensure positive net income.
- Identify prospective donors.
- Research donors.
- Cultivate donor relationships.
- Author and manage the annual appeal.
- Ask donors for major and planned gifts.
- Write foundation and government grants.
- Encourage employee matching gifts.
- Execute fundraising events.
- Steward donors.
- Maintain accurate donor records in the organization's donor management system.

- Recruit, train, supervise, and evaluate fundraising staff.
- Recruit, train, manage, and evaluate fundraising volunteers.
- Staff the development committee.

## Qualifications and Skills

Must have excellent relationship-building, communication, and organization skills. Prefer five years of fundraising experience with progressive levels of responsibilities. Accreditation as a Certified Fundraising Executive (CFRE) is a plus.

# Donor Relationship Manager

## Job Summary

The donor relationship manager oversees all donor fundraising initiatives, including managing donor relationships, interacting with donors to encourage giving, and seeking out sponsorships.

## Responsibilities and Duties

- Identify prospective donors.
- Research donors.
- Cultivate donor relationships.
- Author and manage the annual appeal.
- Ask donors for major and planned gifts.
- Encourage employee matching gifts.
- Steward donors.
- Maintain accurate donor records in the organization's donor management system.

## Qualifications and Skills

Must have excellent relationship-building, communication, and organization skills. Prefer five years of fundraising experience with progressive levels of responsibilities. Certified Fundraising Executive (CFRE) accreditation is a plus.

## Fundraising Assistant

### Job Summary

The fundraising assistant provides administrative support to the development director and staff and participates in all fundraising activities, including donor relations, direct mailings, assembling grant packages, special events, and recordkeeping.

### Responsibilities and Duties

- Assist with general correspondence.
- Assist with preparation for meetings.
- Coordinate and send out mailings.
- Assist with event detail coordination.
- Generate thank-you letters.
- Maintain donor database.
- Run fundraising reports.
- Attend fundraising events to ensure the smooth running of the event.

### Qualifications and Skills

Must exhibit attention to detail. Must have good interpersonal skills. Must be able to prioritize and complete multiple tasks.

# Grant Writer

## Job Summary

The grant writer prepares foundation and government proposals by identifying opportunities and matching them to organizational needs, reviewing requests for proposals and application guidelines, attending funder meetings, formatting information, writing drafts, obtaining approvals, and submitting funding requests.

## Responsibilities and Duties

- Identify potential funding opportunities.
- Research prospects.
- Create an annual grants calendar.
- Author foundation, government, and community group proposals.
- Coordinate program, finance, and administrative efforts around the requirements of specific funders.
- In conjunction with program and finance staff, draft program and grant budgets.
- Assemble and mail grant packages.
- Generate thank-you letters.
- Draft grant reports to funders.
- Draft grant reports to supervisors.
- Maintain accurate records in the donor database.

## Qualifications and Skills

Must have excellent writing and interpersonal skills. Must exhibit good attention to detail. Must be able to conceptualize and organize projects from inception to completion. Must demonstrate the ability to meet multiple deadlines.

# Other Books by Joanne Oppelt

https://amzn.to/3AR9ap4

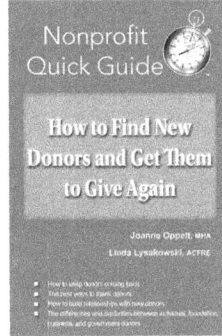

https://amzn.to/2MTcbxZ

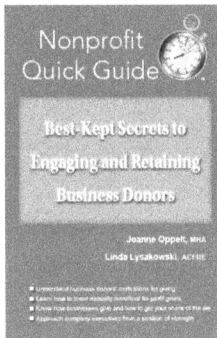

https://amzn.to/2NgdFFO

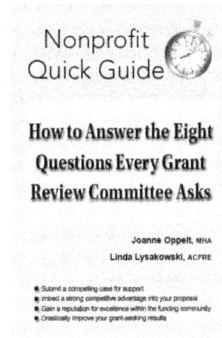

https://amzn.to/3AR9ap4

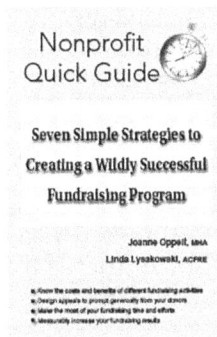

https://amzn.to/3nYdzjP

https://amzn.to/3nYdzjP

https://amzn.to/3myxI1F

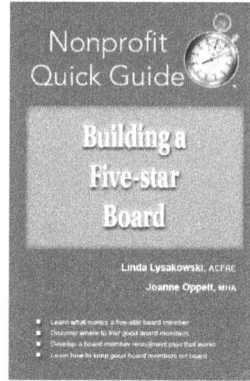

https://amzn.to/347DugS

https://amzn.to/38gASyu

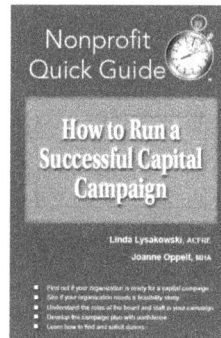

https://amzn.to/2H2Q0FX

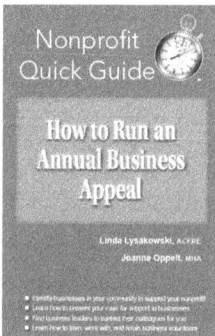

https://amzn.to/3lf5ciG

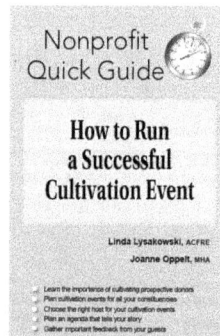

https://amzn.to/37DOdQQ

https://amzn.to/2JXQjmz

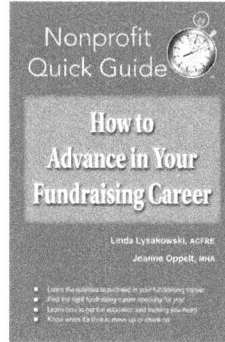

https://amzn.to/2Sgx1ZV

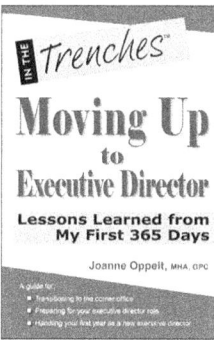

https://amzn.to/38AjdzJ

https://amzn.to/31lJ0e1

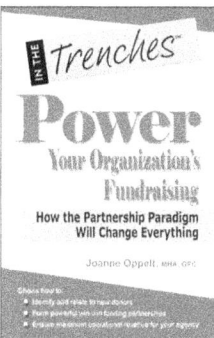

https://amzn.to/2JXQjmz

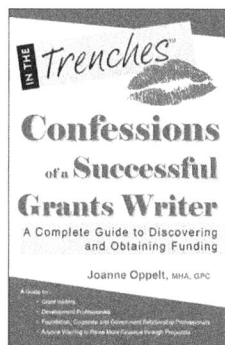

https://amzn.to/3ker0tI

Joanne**Oppelt**

**Seven Simple Strategies to Creating a Wildly Successful Fundraising Program**

## 13 Ten to Twenty-Minute Classes | Private Coaching | Lifetime Access

Create a wildly successful program that generates tremendous fundraising revenues at the least amount of cost.

https://www.joanneoppeltcourses.com/seven-simple-strategies-course-and-coaching-info

Joanne**Oppelt**

How to Answer
the Eight
Questions Every
Grant Review
Committee
Asks

## 11 Ten to Twenty-Minute Classes | Private Coaching | Lifetime Access

Get the insight and skills you need to write compelling proposals that get funded, including crafting grant budgets.

https://www.joanneoppeltcourses.com/eight-questions-course-and-coaching-info

Joanne**Oppelt**

## Best-Kept Secrets to Engaging and Retaining Business Donors

### 14 Ten to Twenty-Minute Online Classes | Private Coaching | Lifetime Access

Penetrate your business community, attract business donors, and get big corporate donations.

https://www.joanneoppeltcourses.com/best-kept-secrets-course-and-coaching-info

# Index

# About Joanne Oppelt Consulting, LLC

Joanne Oppelt Consulting's mission is to help deeply mission-oriented nonprofits build sustainable revenue streams.

## Vision

I envision a world where highly mission-driven organizations are equipped with the tools and infrastructure necessary to financially sustain themselves.

## Values

- Authenticity in all my professional dealings.
- Brutal honesty with myself and my clients, fully disclosing my personal and business approach and interests.
- Two-way ethical transactions in all my business partnerships.
- Fairness in pricing and workload when taking on new clients.
- Partnerships with ethical, top-notch practitioners to provide needed services outside my areas of expertise.
- Engagement in non-political, non-sectarian causes.

https://www.joanneoppeltcourses.com

www.ingramcontent.com/pod-product-compliance
Lightning Source LLC
Chambersburg PA
CBHW061024220326
41597CB00019BB/3327